Non-Invasive Data Governance

Strikes Again

GAINING EXPERIENCE AND PERSPECTIVE

FIRST EDITION

Robert S. Seiner

Technics Publications
SEDONA, ARIZONA

TECHNICS PUBLICATIONS

TECHNOLOGY / LEADERSHIP

115 Linda Vista
Sedona, AZ 86336 USA

https://www.TechnicsPub.com

Edited by Sadie Hoberman

Cover design by Lorena Molinari

First Printing 2023

Copyright © 2023 by Robert S. Seiner

ISBN, print ed.	9781634623599
ISBN, Kindle ed.	9781634623605
ISBN, ePub ed.	9781634623612
ISBN, PDF ed.	9781634623629

Library of Congress Control Number: 2023930977

Too often, data books present a rose-colored lens of how things should be. Bob Seiner certainly has the pedigree to know what needs to change, but he also has the practical experience to make it happen. This book is a key that can help anyone unlock the knowledge that Bob has accumulated the hard way, from the experience of many real-life data governance implementations. Everyone should add this to their data bookshelf, since no matter the scenario, there is likely to be a chapter or essay that will apply and help improve the situation. I can't imagine a better encore to Bob's original Non-Invasive Data Governance book!

Anthony Algmin
Founder, Algmin Data Leadership

In Non-Invasive Data Governance Strikes Again, Bob Seiner reveals to us the many questions an expert must ask to discover the practical path to create a data governance culture of excellence. In this long-awaited sequel to Non-Invasive Data Governance, Bob does not merely update his game changing business book. Bob uncovers, unwraps, exposes, defrags and dissects the lessons and the questions he has discovered in the application of his groundbreaking methodologies for data governance. The reader will be well prepared in a world of generative AI and where companies are inundated with greater volumes of data than ever before. We learn from examples how to manage, steward, measure and to become the best Data Governance professional with the least possible friction.

Michelle Finneran Dennedy
Chief Executive Officer, PrivacyCode, Inc. and Partner, Privatus Strategic Consulting

Bob's invention of the Non-Invasive Data Governance methodology has helped to revolutionize the way organization's manage data. And this book shares the lessons he has learned putting NIDG to practice. So, if you are looking for guidance on governing your organization's data without requiring significant changes to existing processes or infrastructure, let Bob's latest book be your guide.

Craig Mullins
President & Principal Consultant, Mullins Consulting, Inc.

There is not a more prolific source of original ideas in the data governance community than Bob Seiner. He's in the field every day, working alongside his clients to help them address real business opportunities and problems. So, when Bob shares "experience and perspective" in his new book, you are tapping into literally thousands of hours of hard work and creative thinking which have been applied in the real world.

Tony Shaw
CEO and Founder, DATAVERSITY

Bob Seiner's new book, Non-Invasive Data Governance Strikes Again, delivers the right message at the right time for today's data-driven organizations and their data leaders, CIOs, and CDOs. Most importantly, it addresses how to garner program support, demonstrating business value, and the people and technology elements of making it work. As a critical DataOps process, it is time for data governance that actually works.

Myles Suer
Facilitator, CIOChat

Since we've both been involved in Data Governance since its earliest days, my friend Bob Seiner and I have many times been put together on stage to debate implementation approaches. I'd describe leadership-driven efforts focused on big changes, and he'd describe getting started with a non-threatening program that "focuses on leveraging existing levels of accountability while addressing opportunities to improve." During debate, I'd ask him: What comes next? How do you grow such a program? How do you evolve from in-the-trenches attention to details to bigger-picture endeavors? In NIDG Strikes Again! Bob answers those questions, and more.

Gwen Thomas
Founder, The Data Governance Institute and Principal, DGI Consulting

If you enjoyed the practical guidance provided by the first Non-Invasive Data Governance book on creating a formal data governance program, you'll appreciate the valuable insights offered in Non-Invasive Data Governance Strikes Again. This book is a must-read for data practitioners seeking to successfully navigate the multitude of corporate nuances in operationalizing data governance. Drawing on real-world experiences from his consulting practice, Bob Seiner provides readers with a wealth of practical advice on advancing their data governance program to fit their organization's business needs. From securing business sponsorship to measuring the program's business value to designing an effective organizational framework, this book covers it all for data leaders managing a range of data programs. Seiner has compiled these real lessons in essay form since the publication of the first book, providing readers with an updated understanding of data concepts in today's modern workplace.

Peggy Tsai
Chief Data Officer, BigID

CONTENTS

Introduction _____ **1**

Section One: Experience and Perspective _____ **7**

Chapter 1: Lessons Learned _____ **9**

Experience: What is Non-Invasive Data Governance? _____ 10
Experience: The Non-Invasive Data Governance Framework _____ 13
Experience: How is Non-Invasive Data Governance Different? _____ 34
Experience: Comparing Approaches to Data Governance _____ 38
Experience: What Makes a Data Element Critical? _____ 46
Experience: A Data Governance Maturity Model _____ 49

Chapter 2: Perspectives to Consider _____ **55**

Perspective: Fix the "Data Situation" _____ 56
Perspective: Data Governance as a Puzzle _____ 59
Perspective: Data is Like Contaminated Water _____ 66
Perspective: Data Anarchy Versus Governance _____ 68
Perspective: Defeat Your Data Demons _____ 72
Perspective: Your Organization Has the Data Flu _____ 76
Perspective: The Four Horsemen of the Data Apocalypse _____ 79
Perspective: Time for a Data Intervention _____ 83
Perspective: To Own or Not to Own Data _____ 88
Perspective: Truth in Data—Buyer Beware _____ 92

Section Two: Support and Value _____ **97**

Chapter 3: Support and Sponsorship _____ **99**

Experience: CDOs Should Be Asking "How" and Not "Why" _____ 100
Experience: Elements of a Data Strategy _____ 104
Experience: What It Means to Make Data Governance Fun _____ 111
Experience: Calm Management's Fears About Data Governance _____ 117
Perspective: Saving a Failing Data Governance Program _____ 121

Chapter 4: Demonstrating Business Value _____ **127**

Experience: Convincing Stakeholders That Data Governance is Necessary __ 128
Perspective: The Trifecta of People, Process, and Technology _____ 133
Perspective: What You Cannot Do Because Your Data is Ungoverned ___ 137

Experience: Connecting Data to Revenue _____ 140

Experience: Look Out for These Six Data Mistakes _____ 144

Perspective: Ways to Improve Your Data _____ 148

Section Three: Organizations and Roles _____ **151**

Chapter 5: Organizational Design _____ **153**

Experience: Organizational Design and Influence on Program Success _____ 154

Experience: Federating Data Governance _____ 160

Perspective: Who Should Own Data Governance? _____ 167

Perspective: There is Only One Data Governance _____ 171

Perspective: The Same Difference of Data Governance and Data Management _____ 173

Chapter 6: Roles as the Program Backbone _____ **179**

Experience: Data Governance Roles and Responsibilities _____ 180

Perspective: Data is Everybody's Job _____ 191

Perspective: A Steward is a Steward _____ 195

Perspective: What Makes a Data Steward _____ 198

Perspective: Data Stewards Should Get a Raise _____ 201

Experience: Guidelines for Recognizing Data Stewards _____ 203

Experience: A Data Governance Manager Job Description _____ 210

Experience: The Key Role of the Data Governance Partner _____ 215

Section Four: Behavior and Documentation _____ **223**

Chapter 7: Governing People's Behavior _____ **225**

Perspective: The Data Will Not Govern Itself _____ 226

Experience: Change Data Habits Before It is Too Late _____ 229

Experience: Characteristics of Governing Data _____ 235

Experience: Common Data Governance Challenges _____ 240

Perspective: Progressive Principles for Protecting Data _____ 247

Chapter 8: Technology and Metadata _____ **251**

Perspective: Data Governance Challenges Associated with LLMs _____ 252

Experience: Governing Data Mesh and Fabric _____ 261

Experience: Questions Metadata Can Answer _____ 264

Experience: Metadata Tool Requirements _____ 272

Perspective: Metadata Will Not Govern Itself Either _____ 279

Index _____ **283**

Figures

Figure 1-1. Non-Invasive Data Governance Framework _____ 15

Figure 1-2. Completed Non-Invasive Data Governance Framework _____ 16

Figure 1-3. Non-Invasive Data Governance Framework with Levels and Components _____ 23

Figure 1-4. Data Governance Framework Comparison _____ 38

Figure 1-5. Sample Data Management and Data Governance Maturity Model _____ 50

Figure 2-1. Data Sample for Virus Cases_____ 94

Figure 3-1. Partnership Between Data Governance, Data Management, and Information Security _____ 176

Figure 3-2. Data Governance Roles and Responsibilities _____ 180

Figure 4-1. Common Data Governance Challenges_____ 241

Introduction

It has been over eight years since the original version of my book, *Non-Invasive Data Governance: The Path of Least Resistance and Greatest Success*, was published by long-time friend and confidante, Steve Hoberman, and his publishing company, Technics Publications. Since then, there have been five language translations, with more planned for later this year. That demonstrates continued and increasing interest in data governance implementations and approaches that will not be painful or threatening to the organization's culture.

This year was a noteworthy year for organizations implementing formal data governance programs. Although some organizations were very successful, many continue to struggle, which is why we reintroduce the concept of implementing data governance here in a way that is practical and pragmatic, efficient and effective, non-invasive and non-threatening.

The main reason I wrote the first book was to educate people that data governance does not have to be all about "command-and-control." My impression is that people hear the term *data governance* and run for the hills, thinking that someone will tell them how to do their job differently than today and the impact will not be pretty.

You may look at the title of this book as a contradiction of terms. The concept of being non-invasive draws a sharp contrast from the notion of striking anything. The point I am making is that the results of your data governance program must deliver a direct impact on the organization and that you can accomplish formal data governance by taking a less threatening (non-invasive) approach to realize the same or more formal results.

In the first book, I used the expression "recognizing" rather than "assigning" data stewards. I wrote about "formalizing existing accountability" and "applying governance to process." New terminology has entered my dialect over the years, including the statement that "everybody is a data steward, and you must get over that fact" and that "the data (and metadata) will not govern themselves." People are already governing the data of your organization. People are defining, producing, and using data as part of their job. If we hold these people formally accountable for their actions, they are stewards of the data. Non-Invasive Data Governance will assist you with moving from informal to formal accountability.

In this book, I share a series of short essays that address lessons that I have learned over the past ten or more years, ways to make data governance more relatable to non-data people, and perspective I have gained through working with some fantastic organizations.

I have worked in the data management space for many years. The first book focused on selling data governance to your organization so that the higher-ups give the "green light" to proceed with the program's definition, delivery, and administration. The book is about putting the necessary components of data governance into place to deliver successful and sustainable governance in our organization.

The questions typically asked by people selling the need for data governance in their organization are, "What will it take to convince our management to apply resources, time, and money to building and operating a data governance program?" or "How do we get management to understand the importance of data governance?" There are no simple answers to these questions. And the first book is not targeted at specifically answering these questions for your organization.

Each organization has its own way of prioritizing resources, time, and money – determining if data governance is important and valuable enough to pursue – and deciding what will and will not be done.

Instead, I re-offer these words of wisdom to achieve your goals for data governance in your organization with the hope that you consider the non-invasive approach an option. Here are the core set of Messages for Management around Non-Invasive Data Governance from the first book.

Do not sell data governance as being a huge challenge.

If your management already thinks data governance will be a big challenge, assure them that data governance can be implemented in a non-threatening, non-interfering, non-culture changing (dare I say "non-invasive") way to significantly reduce the challenge.

You do not have to implement data governance all at once. In fact, most successful organizations implement their programs incrementally—incrementally in 1) the scope of the data that is governed (domain-wise and organizationally) and/or 2) the level of governance (formal behavior) applied to that data.

Emphasize that data governance is not a technical solution.

There will likely be a technical component to your data governance program. But then again, there might not be. Most people agree that you cannot purchase software or hardware that will be your data governance solution. And most people will agree that organizations can develop simple tools to govern people's behaviors.

Technology can assist in formalizing people's behavior. Data only behaves the way people behave. Therefore, technology may help you govern people's behaviors, but it won't—by itself—govern the data.

Emphasize that people behavior is governed, not data.

Data governance is typically about formalizing the behavior of people for the definition, production, and usage of data. Formalize *people's* behavior, not *data*. Data behaves the way people behave. Therefore, technology may help you govern people's behaviors, but the data does what it's told.

Since people's behavior is governed, many organizations consider data governance to be a process-driven discipline. That is partially true. Getting people to do the right thing at the right time is a big part of governance. However, organizations that "sell" data governance as new "governance processes" struggle because of the inherent (viewed) invasiveness of that approach. Governance should formalize behavior around existing processes first and only add to people's workloads as a last resort.

Emphasize that data governance is an evolution, not a revolution.

As stated earlier, you cannot transition from an ungoverned data environment to a governed data environment all at once. Organizations transition into a governed data state in a few different ways. Some organizations focus early on specific domains or subject areas of data. Some organizations begin by focusing on specific business areas, divisions, units, and systems, rather than implementing their program across the organization. Some organizations focus on critical data and specific critical data elements (CDEs) that impact multiple business units at one time. There is no single correct way to evolve your organization's data governance program. I can almost assure you that if you treat data governance as a revolution, and begin by attempting to govern all of your data at one time, there will be a revolt.

I hope these words of wisdom have caught your eye and that the first book and second and third books soon to come answer your questions about how to stay non-invasive with your approach to data governance.

A special thank you goes out to Ronald Kok (Dutch translation), Nino Letteriello (Italian), Michel Hébert (French), Astrid Gelbke (German), and Michele Iurillo (Spanish)—with more names and languages soon to be added—for approaching my publisher and me to provide this content to people around the world. I am humbled by, and very grateful for, the interest.

Start and stay non-invasive in your approach to data governance.

Experience and Perspective

The Non-Invasive Data Governance approach is older than the first book. The first data governance program I implemented (called stewardship back in the mid-90s) focused on my company's "de-facto" (existing) data stewards – or people in the organization who were already informally responsible for the data. I didn't use the term *non-invasive* at the time and the idea of labeling the de-facto approach as "non-invasive" had not yet come into view.

Back in 2014, I put into words the lessons I learned during that initial implementation as well as several other implementations that followed the same approach over the years. This section of this book focuses on the experience I gained since the first book was published, resulting in an artifact that consolidates these experiences into a working framework. In addition, this section includes ways to evaluate data governance approaches and maturity, and new ways to look at data governance to improve how you speak about the subject with your colleagues.

Lessons Learned

I am always finding new ways to discuss how non-invasive data governance differs from other approaches. I test ways to make the approach stand out and simplify ways to get the core messages and concepts of the approach to be better understood. There are lessons that I have learned about how to further the concept of data governance in general and solidify people's understanding of the benefits of the non-invasive approach.

This chapter describes ways to describe what it means "to govern" and what it means to be "non-invasive," as well as new ways to explain the differences between approaches to data governance. This chapter includes a new framework artifact that pulls together the core components of a successful data governance program while providing an effective way to communicate about the components across the different perspectives of your organization. In addition, this chapter includes thoughts about what makes data critical and provides a maturity model you can use to evaluate and describe your program's present and future states.

Experience: What is Non-Invasive Data Governance?

How the heck can data governance be non-invasive? I am still getting this question a lot these days. In fact, more than 90% of the people that attend my sessions at conferences and on webinars tell me that the term Non-Invasive Data Governance™ is what attracts them to my writings and the session they are attending. They walk out at the end of the sessions as believers. Let me answer this question quickly and to the point:

> *Non-Invasive Data Governance focuses on*
> *formalizing accountability, improving communications, and*
> *cultivating effective cross-organization stewarding of data resources.*

I define data governance as "the execution and enforcement of authority over the management of data and data-related assets." Many organizations view this definition as scary and too aggressive. The truth is that at the end of the day, organizations must "execute and enforce" authority over their data for their data governance program to become and stay effective. I am not saying that you should use this definition, but I do suggest a strong definition to make people lean forward in their chairs to ask what we mean by these words.

I describe Non-Invasive Data Governance as "the practice of applying formal accountability and behavior to assure quality, effective use, compliance, security and protection of data." Non-Invasive describes how governance is applied to ensure the non-threatening management of valuable data assets. The goal is to be transparent, supportive, and collaborative.

Many organizations view data governance as being over-and-above normal work efforts and threatening to the existing work culture of the organization. *It does not have to be that way.*

Many organizations have difficulty getting people to adopt best practices for data governance because of a common belief that data governance is about command-and-control. *It does not have to be that way.*

While I firmly state that data governance is "the execution and enforcement of authority over the management of data," nowhere in that definition does it say that the approach to implementing data governance has to be invasive or threatening to the work, people, and culture of the organization. *It does not have to be that way.*

We can sum up Non-Invasive Data Governance in a few short statements. With Non-Invasive Data Governance:

- Data steward responsibilities are identified and recognized, formalized, and engaged according to their existing responsibility rather than being assigned or handed to people as more work.

- The governance of data is applied to existing policies, standard operating procedures, practices, and methodologies, rather than being introduced or emphasized as new processes or methods.

- The governance of data supports all data integration, privacy, risk management, business intelligence, and master data management activities rather than imposing inconsistent rigor on these initiatives.

- Specific attention is paid to ensuring senior management's understanding of a practical and non-threatening yet effective approach to governing data that will mediate ownership and promote stewarding of data as a cross-organization asset, rather than the traditional method of "you will do this."

- Best practices and key concepts of the non-threatening approach are communicated effectively, compared to the existing practices of identifying and leveraging strengths, and enabling the ability to address opportunities to improve.

Key Messages

By merely including the term "governance", data governance requires the administration of something. In this case, data governance refers to the administering of discipline around the management of data. Rather than making the discipline appear threatening and difficult, I suggest following a Non-Invasive Data Governance approach that focuses on formalizing what already exists and addressing opportunities to improve.

Experience: The Non-Invasive Data Governance Framework

This essay provides a detailed description of a new (since the first book) Non-Invasive Data Governance Framework structure that pulls together many lessons learned over years of implementing the non-invasive approach. The framework is a simple two-dimensional matrix that cross-references the core components of a successful data governance program with the levels (or perspectives) of the organization from the executive to the support levels.

The framework describes the primary components of delivering a successful program and the levels of the organization to which we must apply the components of data governance. The detail of what we consider to deliver a successful program occurs when we address each level (row) for each component (column) in the framework.

The levels of the framework are mostly people- and authority-based. Many organizations use similar definitions of the levels of their organization when it comes to defining how they operate. The levels defined in this framework should look familiar to you if you are acquainted with the Non-Invasive Data Governance Operating Model of Roles and Responsibilities described in my first book, and also updated in this book.

The framework levels are:

- Executive—senior leadership team – enterprise view
- Strategic—business / technology management – business leadership
- Tactical—subject matter expertise – across business areas
- Operational—daily job function – within a business area
- Support—functional management – present governing functions

The framework components are the core moving parts of governance in action for most organizations. The components focus on six basic elements of delivering a successful program. Organizations must focus on the data being governed, the roles people will play, the processes being governed, and how governance is being communicated at all levels of the organization. In addition, organizations must demonstrate business value and make use of technology and tools to govern their data at all levels.

The framework components are:

- Data—assets being governed – structured and unstructured
- Roles—formal accountability and responsibility for data
- Processes—application and enforcement of governance
- Communications—orientation, onboarding, ongoing communications
- Metrics—measures and key performance indicators of program impact
- Tools—artifacts and instruments to enable active governance of data

The Empty Framework

A diagram of an empty Data Governance Framework appears in Figure 1-1. The matrix focuses on the six core components of data governance described above at each of five core levels of the organization. This version of the framework is left blank to emphasize how the cross-section of each component and level is planned, defined, developed, and deployed across the organization.

This diagram does not demonstrate meaning to the organization unless we fill in each of the squares with nouns and verbs representing subjects, actions, artifacts, or messages to consider when planning, defining, developing, and deploying each core component at each respective level.

NON-INVASIVE DATA GOVERNANCE™ FRAMEWORK

Components

	DATA	ROLES	PROCESSES	COMMUNICATIONS	METRICS	TOOLS
EXECUTIVE						
STRATEGIC						
TACTICAL						
OPERATIONAL						
SUPPORT						

Levels

Copyright © 2023 – Robert S. Seiner and KIK Consulting & Educational Services, LLC

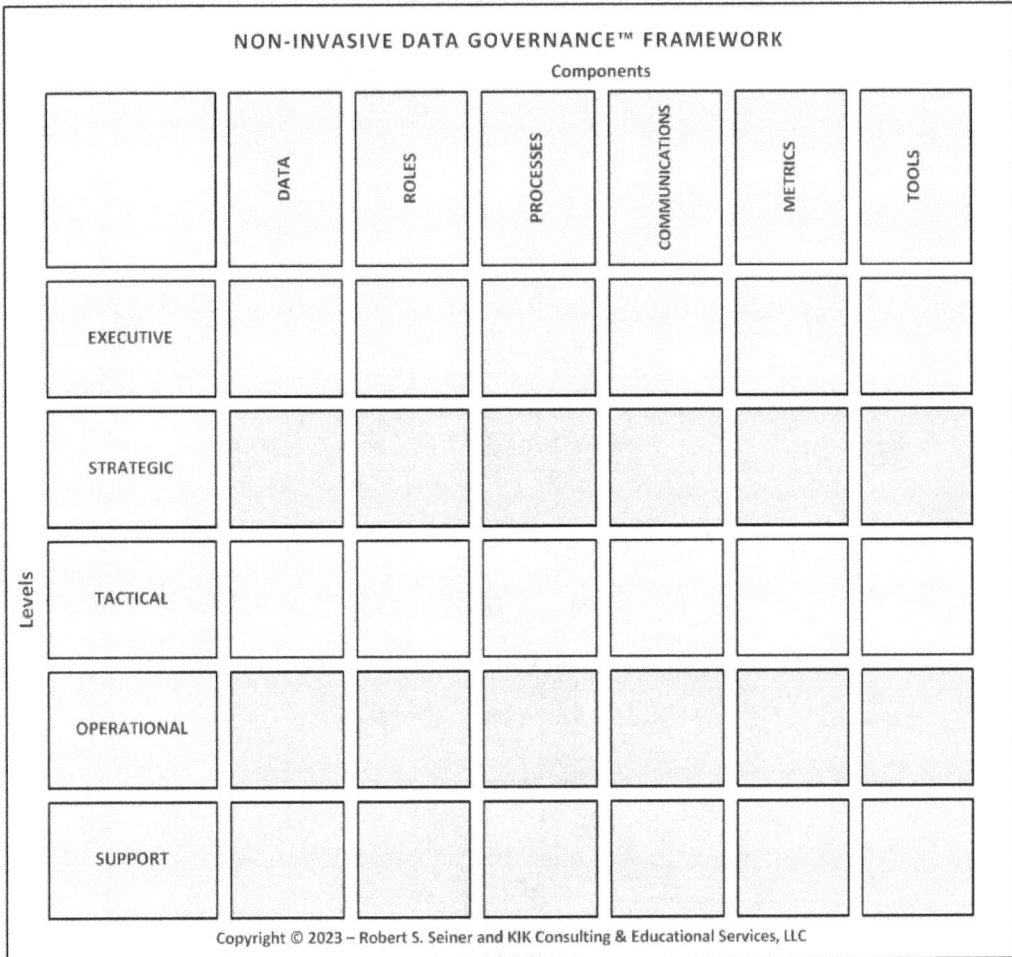

Figure 1-1. Non-Invasive Data Governance Framework

The Completed Framework

Figure 1-2 contains a completed diagram of the Non-Invasive Data Governance Framework. The matrix cross-references each of the six core components of data governance with each of the five core levels of the organization. This version of the framework is completed with nouns and verbs to guide how we plan, define, develop, and deploy each component across the organization.

NON-INVASIVE DATA GOVERNANCE™ FRAMEWORK

Components

	DATA	ROLES	PROCESSES	COMMUNICATIONS	METRICS	TOOLS
EXECUTIVE	Leadership Dashboard KPIs	Leadership Steering Committee	Endorse Enforce Authorize	Support Sponsor Understand	Approve Act	Policy Directive Audit
STRATEGIC	Enterprise Performance	Preside DG Program DG Council	Direct Approve Prioritize Resolve	Status Evaluate Commend	Acceptance Participation Performance	Charter Best Practices Guidelines Roadmap
TACTICAL	Subject Area X-Business Unit	Domain Stewards Data Owners SMEs	Facilitate Mediate Promote	Standards Subject Area Project	Subject Quality Metrics	Standards Requirements Workflows
OPERATIONAL	Business Unit Function	Operational Data Stewards Users	Operate Manage Handle	Orientation Onboard Ongoing	Accountability Efficiency Effectiveness	Glossary Dictionary Catalog Repository
SUPPORT	Accountability Inventory Metadata	Prog Mgmt Admin Work Groups Partners	Formalize Adhere Enforce	Plan Develop Deliver	Collect Report	DG Tools Metadata Tools KIK Artifacts

Levels

Copyright © 2023 – Robert S. Seiner and KIK Consulting & Educational Services, LLC

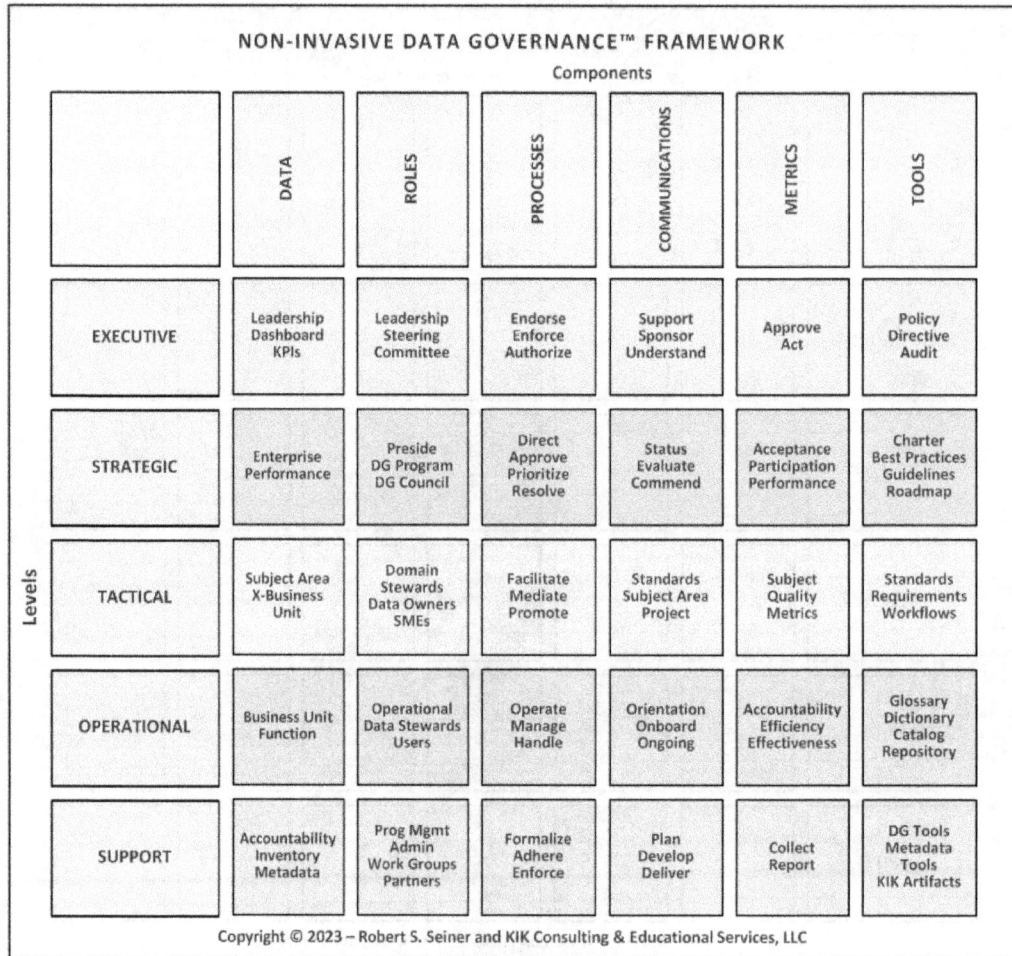

Figure 1-2. Completed Non-Invasive Data Governance Framework

The completed framework demonstrates meaning to the organization by containing points for discussion and planning for the definition, development, and deployment of each core component at each respective level. Figure 1-2 shows the framework completed using terms and phrases that demonstrate how one organization stayed non-invasive in how they completed rthe framework.

The way you complete the framework, including the levels and components you select, and the ways you fill in the empty squares, is entirely up to you. There is no "correct" answer to how to fill it in. Consider completing the empty boxes with terminology and phrases that spell out who, what, why, when and how that component is important at that level.

The Framework Levels (rows)

The levels of the Data Governance Framework represent the levels of the organization. The names given to the levels are typical of many organizations. However, your organization may use different names. Many organizations talk about "right-sizing" the program for their specific needs and using names that closely echo their organizational culture. Also, eliminating or combining levels is more likely than adding levels.

Executive

The executive level of an organization typically consists of people at the top level. This includes boards of directors, presidents, chairs, senior vice presidents, and CXO level positions (meaning CEOs, COOs, CIOs, CDOs, CDAO, CROs, CMOs, etc.). The executive level of an organization often has regular or scheduled meetings as the steering committee for the enterprise.

In Non-Invasive Data Governance (NIDG), data governance is added as a line item on the agenda of regular executive-level meetings. The steering committee includes business and technology leadership for data governance and all other enterprise-level initiatives.

Strategic

The strategic level of an organization typically consists of people that report directly to and are delegated by the executive level to oversee and direct specific initiatives. This can include senior vice presidents, vice presidents, and the people recognized as being second-in-command or representing their part of the organization in the initiative. The strategic level is accountable to the executive level for the success of the initiative.

In NIDG, the strategic level is often labeled as the Data Governance Council. The council's responsibility is to make certain the data governance program is successful. The council is very knowledgeable in the policies and procedures of data governance. It acts as the ultimate decision-maker for resolving issues that could not be resolved at a lower level of the organization.

Tactical

The tactical level of an organization typically consists of people that are subject matter experts, facilitators, and potentially decision makers for specific domains of data and information. The tactical level is delegated or recognized by the strategic level as people who drive data decisions within their domain. The tactical level can be defined through a policy, appointment, or natural selection process (the "go-to person").

In NIDG, the tactical level is often labeled as Data Domain Stewards or Enterprise Data Stewards for a specific subject matter of data. Domain stewards are recognized for their expertise in their subject matter across the enterprise. This role is the most critical role of a NIDG program and can be simple (if people are already seen as subject matter experts) or difficult (there are not obvious people) to fill. Domain stewards can have the authority to make enterprise decisions for their subject matter or they may escalate the decision to the strategic level.

The tactical level may also include Data Owners—although I suggest avoiding using the term "owner" when possible. Ownership implies a highly personal level of control. Stewardship implies a formal but less controlling relationship. I like to use the term Data Domain Steward.

Operational

The operational level of an organization typically consists of every person in the organization that has a relationship with data and is (or will be) held formally accountable for that relationship. The relationships include the definition, production, and/or use of data and information. If an individual does any or all of these activities as part of their job, this individual must be expected to follow policy, best practices, and standards for that relationship.

In NIDG, the operational level can include everybody in the organization. These people are known as the true stewards of the data or people who are formally accountable for how they define, produce, and use data. These people do not require a title of data steward. From the operational level up through the framework hierarchy, people must be held formally accountable for their actions associated with the data. In NIDG, specific and thorough attention is paid to governance awareness at all levels, whether that awareness focuses on quality, protection, or management of the data.

Support

The support levels of an organization typically include the people responsible for the data governance program, the supporting knowledge of Information Technology (IT), Project Management Office (PMO), regulatory and compliance groups, information security, legal and audit, communications, human resources, and working groups assembled to address issues and opportunities. That is, any group actively governing something or with a vested interest in the "execution and enforcement of authority over the management of data.

In NIDG, the support level varies with the program design in each organization. Leadership of the data governance program is the critical level of support, and the support and involvement of IT and the PMOs act as stalwart contributors to the most successful programs.

The Framework Components (columns)

The components of the Non-Invasive Data Governance Framework are the core pieces of putting together a successful data governance program. The core components are critical pieces that the program cannot do without. Many practitioners discuss people, processes, and technology as the linchpins of a successful program. I have added three components and provide a different way to display the technology.

Data

The first foundational component of the NIDG Framework focuses on the scope of the resources to govern. Disciplines such as records, document, and information management may exist, and the framework can be used to differentiate between the data, information, records, and knowledge needs at all levels of the organization.

In NIDG, the approach to governance is very similar across each of the different data resources, including the execution and enforcement of authority and the formalization of accountability for the data resources that are in scope.

Roles

The second component of a successful data governance program is the definition of roles and responsibilities. How roles are defined predicts the effort required to govern the data. Assignment into roles often presents pushback when the effort is over-and-above existing responsibilities. Identification into roles encounters less pushback as people see themselves in the roles that they have been slotted. The recognition of people into roles is a direct manner of acknowledgment of the part each person plays in the program.

In NIDG, we typically represent roles through a NIDG Operating Model of Roles and Responsibilities (described later in this book). An operating model must describe formalized responsibilities, escalation, and decision paths, how roles are formally engaged in processes, and communications shared with each level.

Processes

The third component focuses on applying roles to processes. The notion of a single "data governance process" misrepresents that processes are a primary component of data governance success. Instead, we apply data governance to a series of processes.

In NIDG, we pay attention to providing repeatable processes that reflect the appropriate level of formal accountability throughout the process.

Data governance focuses on getting the "right" person involved in the "right" step of the process to deliver the "right" result regardless of the process focus— issue resolution, protection, quality, project-focused.

Data governance becomes the application of formal governance to process.

Communications

Communication is a vital component of a successful data governance program. Raising the data awareness and literacy of every person who defines, produces, and uses data is critical to achieving program success. In addition, education must focus on policies, handling rules, best practices, standards, processes, and role-based governance activities.

In NIDG, communications play a role in every aspect of program definition and delivery. Communications must be thorough and measurable. Communications must focus on formalizing accountability for issue resolution, data protection, quality improvement, or any other application of authority for managing data.

The communications plan must mirror the roles component described in the framework. In addition, communications must include orientation, on-boarding, and discussions of relevant subjects focused on the specific audience while utilizing available communication instruments.

Metrics

Data governance programs must be able to measure their impact on the organization. The impact and value may not always be financially quantifiable. Measuring efficiency and effectiveness improvements require benchmarks of the present state and the governed activity of measuring and reporting results.

In NIDG, organizations measure improvements in governance by collecting and reporting the number of issues reported and resolved, the number of people engaged, the amount of data that has been "certified," and the number of standards and policies that are known and followed.

When requested, data governance metrics and measurements must be auditable and verifiable to management and authorities. Organizations typically count the reusability and understandability of data definitions, the ability and speed to access the "right" data at the "right" time, the production of high-quality data, and the proper usage and handling of data.

Tools

Tools of data governance enable the program to deliver value to the organization. Organizations use tools they develop internally as well as tools that they've purchased to fill specific needs of their programs. The tools developed or purchased are based on practicality, ease of use, and the specific goals of the data governance program.

In NIDG, tools formalize accountability for managing data and improving the inventories and knowledge of the data, rules, and processes required to govern data. Tools record and make available metadata to improve the understanding and quality of data across the enterprise.

The data governance tools market is growing as the definition of data governance expands to address authority enforcement over big data, smart data, metadata, and all data used for analytics. Before investing in new technologies, organizations should clearly state their requirements, consider leveraging existing tools, and develop tools internally to address specific metadata needs of their data governance program.

The remainder of this essay focuses on the completing the empty squares of the framework with nouns and verbs that provide direction for meaningful discussions about how the program will be set up and operate. Consider focusing on the stakeholder perspectives that will derive value from following the Non-Invasive Data Governance approach.

NON-INVASIVE DATA GOVERNANCE™ FRAMEWORK

Components

	DATA	ROLES	PROCESSES	COMMUNICATIONS	METRICS	TOOLS
EXECUTIVE	Leadership Dashboard KPIs	Leadership Steering Committee	Endorse Enforce Authorize	Support Sponsor Understand	Approve Act	Policy Directive Audit
STRATEGIC	Enterprise Performance	Preside DG Program DG Council	Direct Approve Prioritize Resolve	Status Evaluate Commend	Acceptance Participation Performance	Charter Best Practices Guidelines Roadmap
TACTICAL	Subject Area X-Business Unit	Domain Stewards Data Owners SMEs	Facilitate Mediate Promote	Standards Subject Area Project	Subject Quality Metrics	Standards Requirements Workflows
OPERATIONAL	Business Unit Function	Operational Data Stewards Users	Operate Manage Handle	Orientation Onboard Ongoing	Accountability Efficiency Effectiveness	Glossary Dictionary Catalog Repository
SUPPORT	Accountability Inventory Metadata	Prog Mgmt Admin Work Groups Partners	Formalize Adhere Enforce	Plan Develop Deliver	Collect Report	DG Tools Metadata Tools KIK Artifacts

Levels (vertical label on left)

Copyright © 2023 – Robert S. Seiner and KIK Consulting & Educational Services, LLC

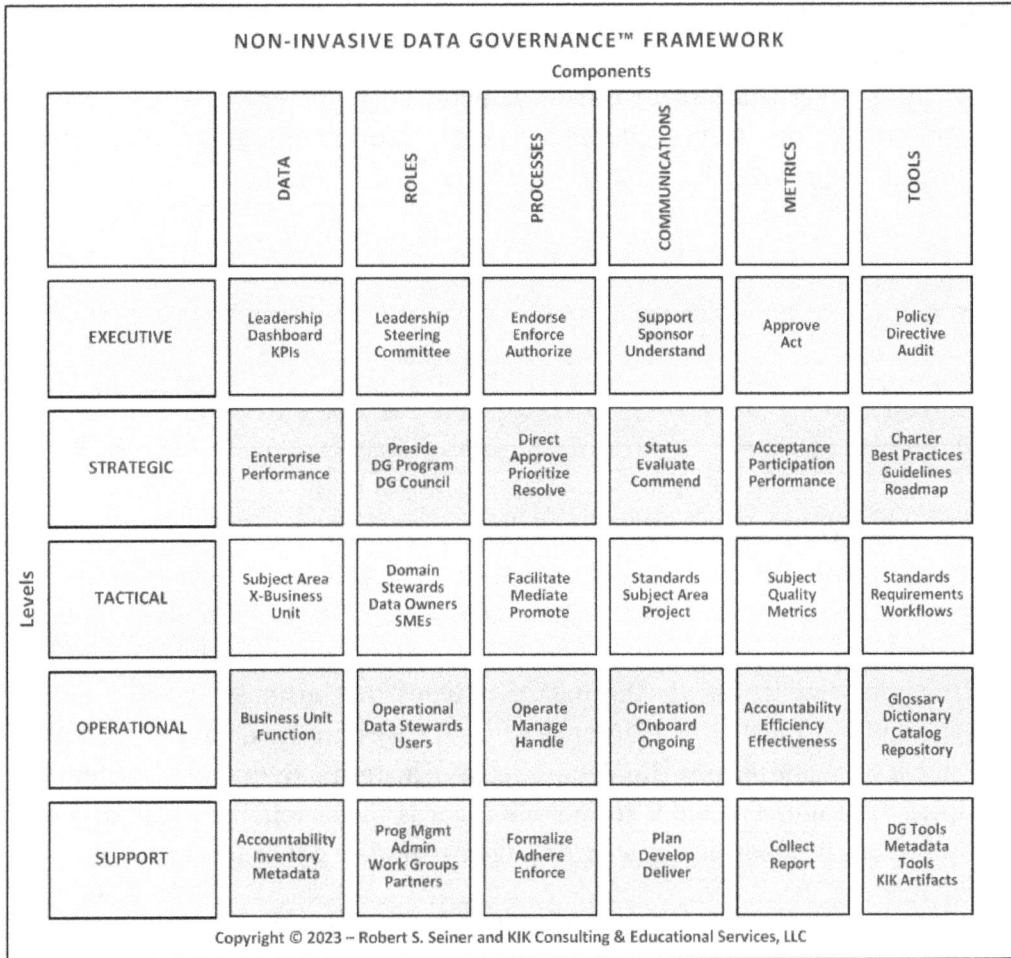

Figure 1-3. Non-Invasive Data Governance Framework with Levels and Components

---

Data by Level

The data itself is the first foundational component of a successful data governance program. When using the term data, we include structured data that exists within databases and information systems, and unstructured data which can include any data not traditionally stored within a database or file such as documents, content, audio, video, and records that require governance. The use of the term "records" is the vaguest and least understood of the data types, although the discipline has been around longer in many organizations. The type of data governed often dictates the name of the program—data governance, information governance, records management, and even metadata governance. I will not resolve the difference between data, information, and records in this framework but realize the framework addresses the core components of all of these categories of data.

In NIDG, there are two main focuses.
The data you select to govern and the people you select to govern the data.

Non-Invasive Data Governance programs do not have to begin by focusing on all of the different types of data suggested here. Traditionally, data governance programs have (at least initially) focused on the data in systems developed, purchased, and implemented by the IT part of the organization or within a specific department. This is the data that feeds the business intelligence and analytical platforms. Data governance often focuses on the data in systems and the metadata that explains the data. The Information Governance discipline is acknowledged more recently to include records management, which as a data discipline, has been around as long or longer than data governance.

Executive Level: Leadership Dashboard KPIs	People at the executive level focus on the data that enables them to be effective leaders of the organization. Often, this data is provided in summary and/or graphical form through dashboards and reports, or through self-service portals that focus the data on a task at hand. Structured data is mainly consumed at this level for decision-making and unstructured data for conditional purposes.
Strategic Level: Enterprise Performance	The data governance council (or similarly named committee) ensures that the program is designed, developed, deployed, and maintained to provide measurable value to the organization through improved performance and other metrics. The council is focused on the data, information, records, and metadata that the organization needs to become efficient and effective in managing the data as an asset. That asset can include structured and unstructured data, records, and metadata.

Tactical Level: Subject Area Cross Business Unit	The people participating in your program's tactical level roles have formal accountability for data within a specific subject area or function. People at the tactical level have formal accountability for that data across business units or functional areas of the organization. The tactical stewards (often referred to as data domain stewards) are formally accountable for how the data in their subject matter is defined, produced, and used. This data can include structured or unstructured data as well as records about the domain.
Operational Level: Business Unit Function	Operational data is what drives the business and keeps it functioning. This data can include structured and unstructured data, records, and metadata that the people in the business units use to perform their functions efficiently and effectively. The data defined, produced, and used by the business begins the pipeline to feed the data to the executive level.
Support Level: Accountability Inventory Metadata	The support areas of the program, referred to as partners, provide their perspective through the function they serve. For example, IT security as a partner focuses on the security discipline associated with their function. The administration of the program requires governed metadata that assists in formalizing accountability, and inventorying the data, data stewardship, and views of all aspects of the data, whether that is structured or unstructured, from defining the data to producing the data to using of the data.

Roles by Level

The second foundational component of a successful data governance program is the definition of roles and responsibilities. How we define roles predicts the effort required to govern the data. Assignment into roles often presents pushback when the effort is considered over-and-above existing responsibilities. Identification into roles encounters less pushback as people already see themselves in their slotted roles. Recognition of people into roles is a direct manner of acknowledgment of each person's part in the program.

In NIDG, we represent the data governance roles through the NIDG Operating Model of Roles and Responsibilities. The familiar pyramid diagram from the first NIDG book is also updated and represented in the essay Data Governance Roles and Responsibilities in chapter six.

A complete operating model provides a detailed description of formalized responsibilities, escalation, and decision paths, how roles are formally engaged in processes, who typically participates in the role and how much of their time is typically required, and communications shared with each level.

Executive Level: Leadership Steering Committee	The steering committee's role is to sponsor, approve, understand, and champion the enterprise strategic data governance plan and policy at the highest level of the organization, such as the executive or leadership level. The committee must communicate effectively with lines of business on the expectations and requirements for governing data and identify and prioritize data initiatives. This will require significant education and understanding on the part of your organization's executives. The committee delegates responsibility for strategic decision making to the Data Governance Council.
Strategic Level: Preside DG Program DG Council	The Data Governance Council's role is to become educated in what data governance means, how it can and will work for the organization, and what it means to embrace and activate the data stewards. The council provides guidance, presides over program activities, and approves data policy, methods, priorities, and tools. The council promotes governance in their areas by actively engaging in improved data practices. The council makes timely data decisions at a strategic level given the appropriate knowledge to make that decision, and meets regularly to stay informed of program activities.
Tactical Level: Domain Stewards Data Owners SMEs	The domain steward (often referred to as Owner or Subject Matter Expert—SME) focuses on the quality, value, and protection of data that falls under a specific domain (subject area) for the enterprise. We identify these people most-often by position, and they are the facilitators in cross-business resolution of data issues within their domain. The domain steward may or not be the authority (decision-maker), depending on their position in the organization. The domain steward is responsible for escalating well-documented issues to the strategic level, documenting data classification rules, compliance rules, and business rules for data in their domain. In addition, the domain steward often participates in tactical work groups for finite periods to address specific issues, opportunities, and projects related to their domain.

Operational Level: Operational Data Stewards Users	The operational-level data steward's role is to demonstrate accountability for their relationship to the data they define, produce, and use daily. The data stewards are educated and often certified as knowing the rules associated with data they define, produce, and use.
Support Level: Program Management Administration Work Groups Partners	It is the role of the support areas of the organization, including data governance management and their team, and partners across the organization, including information technology, information security, audit, legal, risk management, and project management (to name several), to administer and support the activities of the data governance program by being a part of working groups and participating in appropriate governing activities for their support areas.

Processes by Level

The third foundational component of a successful program is the way people are recognized into roles and how the roles are applied to processes. The notion of the "data governance process" misrepresents the fact that processes are a primary component of data governance success. There is not a single process that is governed; rather, there are a series of processes to which we apply data governance.

In NIDG, data governance programs typically provide repeatable processes that reflect the appropriate level of formal accountability throughout the process. Data governance focuses on getting the "right" person involved in the "right" step of the process to deliver the "right" result, regardless of the process focus—issue resolution, protection, quality, project-focused—data governance becomes the application of formal governance to processes. In NIDG, governance is applied to processes rather than there being a data governance process.

Executive Level: Endorse Enforce Authorize	The executive level must know about the processes and how they are governed. The executive level should understand the impact of governing the process, the required resources, and the reasonable expectations for the value this will bring to the enterprise. Once the executive level has this understanding, it is their responsibility to endorse, enforce, support, sponsor, and authorize the governed processes.
Strategic Level: Direct Approve Prioritize Resolve	The strategic level takes the executive endorsement of governed processes to an actionable level. The strategic level identifies and oversees the data governance team's activities, key processes, and players at the tactical level. The council resolves process issues brought to them for strategic decision-making and meets regularly to direct, approve, review, and prioritize data governance process activities.
Tactical Level: Facilitate Mediate Promote	The tactical level is closely engaged in managing data domains (subject areas) by utilizing enterprise Subject Matter Experts (SMEs). The tactical level initiates, facilitates, and mediates the resolution of cross-business area processes and data issues regarding their area of expertise. The tactical level promotes, directs, and coordinates the operational level activities of stewards in their part of the organization and escalates issues to the strategic level as necessary.
Operational Level: Operate Manage Handle	The operational level is engaged daily in governed processes defined at the tactical level and enforced at the strategic level. The operational level is educated and certified in following the processes and rules associated with managing the data (defining, producing, and using data). The operational level reports changes in efficiency and effectiveness to the tactical level to drive continual process improvement and follows the rules associated with handling classified information.
Support Level: Formalize Adhere Enforce	The support level formalizes and enforces the governed processes. The support level includes the data governance team, information security, risk and compliance, project management, legal/audit, and other partners that ensure that processes are adhered to and enforced through education and technology.

Communications by Level

The fourth foundational component, Communications, is a very important piece of a successful data governance program. Raising the data awareness of every person that defines, produces, and uses data is critical to achieving program success. In addition, education must focus on policies, handling rules, best practices, standards, processes, and role-based governance activities.

In NIDG, communications play a role in every aspect of a program's definition and delivery. Communications must be thorough and measurable. Communications must focus on formalizing accountability for the processes mentioned above: issue resolution, protection, quality, project-focused, or any other application of authority in managing data.

The communications plan must mirror the roles component described in this framework. Communications must include orientation, on-boarding, and ongoing discussions focused on the specific audience (executive, strategic, tactical, operational, and support) utilizing available communication instruments.

Executive Level: Support Sponsor Understand	Best practice dictates that the executive level support, sponsor, and, most importantly, understand, how data governance works and what it will take to be successful in the organization. To achieve this, the communications plan plays an important role. Governance information must be shared effectively to resonate and become adopted at the executive level. The executive level will only support and sponsor data governance if they understand the who, what, why, where, and when concerning how the NIDG program will proceed.
Strategic Level: Status Evaluate Commend	The strategic level receives regular (scheduled) communications on governed process status. The strategic level evaluates and approves detailed governance policy and practices by regularly reviewing program communications and status. The strategic level pushes communications into their business areas, commends improvements in efficiency and effectiveness, and supports governed activities.

Tactical Level: Standards Subject Area Project	Governance communications focus on subject areas of data and the standards, rules, and processes associated with defining, producing, and using data in the tactical domains. In addition, the tactical level is involved in developing education, awareness, and governance materials focused on their subject area of data, for subject area projects and related processes across the organization.
Operational Level: Orientation Onboarding Ongoing	The operational level receives communications on how they will be formally held accountable for governing data. The operational level follows the approved rules and governed processes while monitoring and reporting governance results. The operational level is oriented to data governance, brought onboard at the appropriate time, and receives ongoing communications associated with governing data.
Support Level: Plan Develop Deliver	The support level, including all organization governance-style functions, communicates appropriate formal behavior advocated by their function. The support level coordinates with the data governance team to plan, develop, and deliver thorough current and regular communications about governing data.

Metrics by Level

The fifth foundational component of a NIDG program is metrics. Data governance programs must be able to measure their impact on the organization. This is often the responsibility of the support role, often called the Data Governance Manager, Administrator, Lead and/or Team. The impact and value of data governance may be financially quantifiable—but this may not always be the case. Measuring efficiency and effectiveness improvements requires benchmarks of the present state, as well as the governed activity of measuring and reporting results.

In NIDG, organizations measure improvements in governance by collecting and reporting the number of issues recorded and addressed, as well as changes that positively impact the efficiency and effectiveness of business functions. Organizations must also quantify the value of issue resolution, education, awareness, and certification of handling rules and incidents.

When requested, data governance metrics and measurements must be auditable and verifiable to management and authorities. Organizations typically count the reusability and understandability of data definitions, the ability and speed to access the "right" data at the "right" time, the production of high-quality data, and the proper usage and handling of data.

Executive Level: **Approve** **Act**	The executive level reviews and approves how to implement governance and how to measure value across the organization. In addition, the executive level receives results from the strategic, tactical, and support levels, and acts to improve governance capabilities.
Strategic Level: **Acceptance** **Participation** **Performance**	The strategic level works with the tactical and support levels to define and deliver acceptable processes to measure data governance. The strategic level promotes active benchmarking and delivering measurable metrics and business value to the executive level. Typical metrics focus on the acceptance of the program by the organization, participation of business functions and key participants, and performance of the organization.
Tactical Level: **Subject** **Quality Metrics**	The tactical level defines how to measure governance in relation to domain-level quality requirements and the need to protect data in that domain or subject area. The tactical level delivers metrics associated with domain-focused quality of data definition, production, and usage across the organization.
Operational Level: **Accountability** **Efficiency** **Effectiveness**	We measure the operational level in terms of accountability, efficiency, and effectiveness in defining, producing, and using data throughout their daily processes. The operational level follows process and procedure to define, collect, report, and analyze the value of governance to the organization's operations, individuals, and teams.
Support Level: **Collect** **Report**	Each support level area's responsibility is to define, collect, and report effective metrics and measurements to demonstrate the governance value of the function they are providing to the organization. Value will include improvement in business operations, reduction of risk, and the ability to protect data, as well as improvements in the value received from the data and improved analytical capabilities.

Tools by Level

The final foundational component of a NIDG program is tools. Tools of data governance enable the program to deliver value to the organization. Organizations use tools they develop internally, as well as tools that they've purchased to fill specific needs of their programs. Tools that are developed or purchased are based on practicality, ease-of-use, and specific goals of the data governance program.

In NIDG, tools formalize accountability for managing data and improving the knowledge of the data, rules, and processes required to govern data. In addition, tools record and make available metadata to improve the understanding and quality of data across the enterprise. The data governance tools market is growing as the definition of data governance expands to address authority enforcement over big data, smart data, metadata, and data used for analytics. Before investing in new technologies, organizations should clearly state their requirements, consider leveraging existing tools, and develop tools internally to address the specific metadata needs of their data governance program.

Executive Level: **Policy** **Directive** **Audit**	The executive level is responsible for issuing the directive to govern data across the organization. This directive may take the form of policy and written statements outlining the executive level's support, sponsorship, and understanding of the core and guiding principles of data governance and the approach the organization will follow. In addition, a dashboard for governance and audit results delivery to the executive level is valuable for program sustenance.
Strategic Level: **Charter** **Best Practices** **Guidelines** **Roadmap**	The tools of the strategic level are artifacts that are put in place to establish formal data governance in the organization. The strategic level is responsible for accepting governance best practices and assessing and critically analyzing how the organization compares to the best practices and guidelines. The strategic level accepts the action plan and roadmap for aligning the organization with proposed data governance best practices and supports the organization's tactical, operational, and support levels to achieve a best practice state.

Tactical Level: Standards Requirements Workflow	The tools of the tactical level include approved data quality standards and requirements for improving the governance of data per domain across the organization. In addition, the tactical level is responsible for developing and promoting data requirements, standards, and governed workflows to the strategic level for approval and enforcement by the support level of the program.
Operational Level: Glossary Dictionary Catalog Repository	The operational level uses metadata tools to improve their ability to define, produce, and use data as part of their daily job. The operational level provides business definitions of data used to build business glossaries, data dictionaries, data catalogs, and other metadata resources and repositories. In addition, the operational level assists in mapping data meaning and legacy across disparate information systems and data stores.
Support Level: DG Tools Metadata Tools KIK Artifacts	The support level delivers tools associated with their business function, including software focused on improving the Information Technology, Information Security, Risk and Compliance, Audit, Legal, and Project Management functions. The data governance administrator and team use vendor-provided tools, customizable templates, metadata tools, and models to improve their program's performance and maximize data governance's value.

Key Messages

The framework shared here details the foundational components and organizational levels to ensure success with your NIDG program. There are many approaches to data governance. If you are not implementing data governance in a non-invasive manner, I hope the framework includes ideas that can further your data governance discipline and provide additional successes to complement your program.

Experience: How is Non-Invasive Data Governance Different?

No one needs to tell you that data and information are a big part of your life. From the personal data you meticulously manage to the data you have about your customers, products, and suppliers. From the services you provide to the data you protect, analyze, and report personally or through your business. From the proper, moral, and legal responsibility for the formal accountability of every person in your organization to appropriately managing that data. These things define "data governance."

Data can 1) be of great value to the organization or 2) data can be the one thing that stands in the way of the viability and ability of your organization to best serve its customers or stay one step ahead of its competitors.

Businesses and organizations recognize that data is a valuable asset and potential liability at the highest levels of these entities. A way exists to formally govern your data without interfering with the present business plans, upsetting the culture, and threatening the people who already define, produce, and use data to perform their work functions.

As you know, I refer to this approach as *Non-Invasive Data Governance*. Data governance programs focus on the execution and enforcement of authority and accountability for managing data as a valued organizational asset. Data governance programs focus on managing risk and maximizing the organization's data and information value. In this "big data" age, a real definition for data governance could include "formalizing people's behavior through the application of proper accountability for their relationship with the data—leading to improvements in data risk management, increased quality and understanding of data, and improved analytical and decision-making capabilities."

In other words, data governance exemplifies everything a business or organization needs to succeed and prosper. Data governance leads to the formal management of data as a strategic organizational asset, and the formal stewardship of and accountability for data across an organization. As a result, many organizations are considering data governance program implementations if they have not already started down this path. The following table outlines the core difference between the Non-Invasive Data Governance approach and traditional methods of implementing data governance:

With Non-Invasive Data Governance:	With other approaches to data governance:
Data governance is communicated as something already taking place, albeit in an informal, inefficient, and often ineffective manner. Non-Invasive Data Governance focuses on formalizing existing levels of accountability, addressing lapses in formal accountability, and typically costs the time that is put into the effort.	Data governance is communicated as being expensive, complex, time-consuming and over-and-above the existing work culture of the organization.
Non-Invasive Data Governance is viewed as being designed to fit the organization's culture and to take advantage of existing levels of governance so as to not be viewed as encroachment.	Data governance is viewed as a discipline that will add unnecessary rigor and bureaucracy to business processes, thus slowing delivery cycles and making data more difficult to access and use.
Non-Invasive Data Governance expectations are set by assisting business areas to recognize and articulate what they cannot do because the organization's data will not support those activities.	Data governance expectations are set by the team of individuals responsible for designing and implementing the data governance program.
Individuals are identified and recognized into roles associated with their existing relationship to the data, as data definers, producers, users, subject matter experts, and decision-makers, to stress their importance and impact on data across the organization.	Individuals are assigned new roles as part of their involvement in the data governance program.
Individual job titles do not change, and there is an acknowledgment that the vast majority of their responsibilities will not change.	Individuals are given the title of data steward and their job responsibilities are adjusted accordingly.
More than one data steward (formally accountable person) is associated with each type of data. The organization recognizes numerous people with this association to data (i.e., multiple	Individuals are assigned as THE data steward for specific subject areas of data (i.e., a customer data

With Non-Invasive Data Governance:	With other approaches to data governance:
users of particular data that all must be held formally accountable for how they use the data).	steward, a product data steward, finance data steward).
Organizations apply Non-Invasive Data Governance principles to existing workflows and processes by formalizing discipline, accountability, and involvement in these processes.	Organizations refer to processes as "data governance processes" giving the impression that the processes are being carried out because of or as a result of the data governance program.
Non-Invasive Data Governance can be managed out of a business unit or Information Technology unit as both the business areas and IT hold specific knowledge and formal accountability relative to governing data as a valued enterprise effort.	Data governance must reside in a business unit and be directed as a business effort with limited involvement from Information Technology.

With Non-Invasive Data Governance:

- Data steward responsibilities are identified, recognized, formalized, and engaged according to their existing responsibility rather than assigned or handed to people as more work. Everybody is a steward.

- Data governance is applied to existing policies, standard operating procedures, practices, and methodologies—rather than being introduced or emphasized as new processes or methods.

- The governance of data augments and supports all data integration, privacy, risk management, business intelligence, and master data management activities rather than imposing inconsistent rigor to these initiatives.

- Specific attention is paid to ensuring senior management's understanding of a practical and non-threatening yet effective approach to governing data to mediate ownership and promote stewarding of data as a cross-organization asset, rather than the traditional method of "you will do this."

Communicate where you compare to best practice.
Then leverage your strengths and address your opportunities to improve.

Key Messages

By merely including the term "governance," data governance requires the administration of something. In this case, data governance refers to the administering of discipline around the management of data. Rather than making the discipline appear threatening and difficult, I suggest following a Non-Invasive Data Governance approach to formalize what already exists and address opportunities to improve.

Experience: Comparing Approaches to Data Governance

There are three approaches to implementing data governance. The approaches include the Command-and-Control approach, the Traditional approach, and the Non-Invasive Data Governance approach. This essay quickly summarizes each approach and compares how organizations apply them. The method to compare the approaches focuses on the six core components of a data governance program that I addressed in the Non-Invasive Data Governance Framework.

DATA GOVERNANCE FRAMEWORK COMPARISON
Governance Approaches

Components	COMMAND and CONTROL	TRADITIONAL	NON-INVASIVE
DATA	Data	Data Information	Data Information Records Knowledge
ROLES	Assign Roles	Identify Roles	Recognize Formalize Roles
PROCESS	New Process	Single Process	Apply to Process
COMMUNICATIONS	You Will Do This	You Should Do This	You Already Do This
METRICS	Measure Financial Value	Measure Data Quality	Measure Formality & Advancement
TOOLS	Purchase First	Leverage Existing	Leverage Build Purchase

Copyright © 2023 – Robert S. Seiner and KIK Consulting & Educational Services, LLC

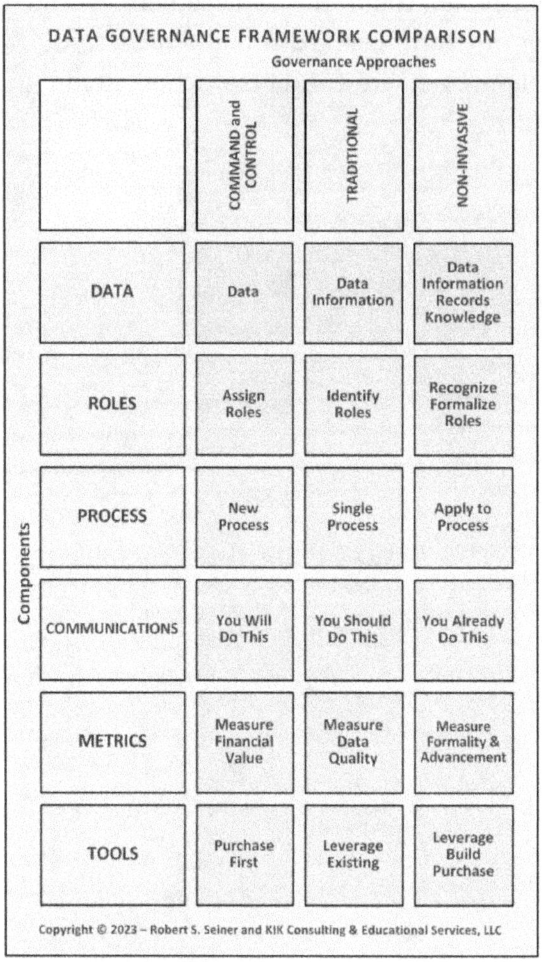

Figure 1-4. Data Governance Framework Comparison

The Command-and-Control Approach

The Command-and-Control Data Governance Approach is primarily a top-down method that begins with the requirement for the governance of data coming as a mandate from leadership of the organization or as a response to an internal or external report from an examiner or auditor.

Characteristics of the Command-and-Control approach include:

- Data in databases, systems, and analytical data resources are the entire focus of the program.

- People are ASSIGNED new responsibilities that feel over-and-above existing responsibilities.

- People are told that governance is a NEW PROCESS that must be applied to solve issues and address opportunities.

- People are told that the governance activities WILL fit in among existing priorities.

- The program is measured on Return on Investment (ROI) and bottom-line impact.

- Governance tools, such as catalogs and repositories, are a primary focus of the program.

The Traditional Approach

The Traditional Governance Approach follows a refrain of "if you build it, they will come." Programs traditionally build the necessary program components, like the roles and the tools, with the hopes and expectations that people will move toward participating in the roles and utilizing the tools. The success of traditional programs depends on program management's ability to get people to participate and use the tools.

Characteristics of the Traditional approach include:

- All data is in scope, including structured and unstructured data, however, it cannot all be addressed at the same time.

- People are IDENTIFIED into governance roles based on existing responsibilities.

- People are told that governance is THE process that is applied across a variety of business needs.

- People are told that the governance activities SHOULD be fit in among existing priorities.

- The program is measured based on improvements in the dimensions of data quality.

- Governance tools are a primary focus of the program, with emphasis placed on building internal tools before buying them.

The Non-Invasive Approach

The Non-Invasive Data Governance Approach emphasizes that there are levels of governance already in place that can be leveraged toward the effective governance of data. People already define, produced, and use data as part of their jobs. In many organizations, people have informal accountability for the data they define, produce, and use – meaning that there are not consistent or formal guidelines for how these actions take place.

Characteristics of the Non-Invasive approach include:

- All data is in scope and the program recognizes pre-existing governance may already be taking place under different names (Information Governance, Records, Document, and Content Management).

- People are RECOGNIZED into governance roles based on existing responsibilities. Assistance, in the form of governance components, is provided to those with relationships to data.

- People are told that governance is something that is APPLIED TO processes rather than redefining a process that is being followed. Governance involves getting the "right" people involved at the "right" time.

- People are told that the governance activities ARE ALREADY PART of their existing priorities and that the program enables them to define, produce, and use quality data.

- The program is measured based on return on investment from all primary information and data technology activities of the organization rather than the program itself. Value is based on the business outcomes of focused data endeavors and projects that are being completed.

- Governance tools are an enabler of program success, with emphasis placed on aligning new tools and tools in your environment with well-defined business and technical metadata requirements.

In the balance of this essay, I will run through each of the components of the Non-Invasive Data Governance framework that was shared earlier in this book and provide a quick statement of how each component is typically viewed for each of the three approaches.

Data

In a *Command-and-Control* approach to data governance, data that resides in databases and structured (and modeled) data resources are at the core of all discussions. Organizations recognize data is important to people at all levels of the organization, and the emphasis is on delivering data from those databases and resources to the end-user community.

In a *Traditional* approach to data governance, the term "data" refers to structured and unstructured data. Organizations define the differences between "data" and "information" often providing separate functions for Data and Information Governance.

In a *Non-Invasive* approach to data governance, it is common for organizations to blend the functions of Data and Information Governance under the name of data governance while also including the governance of structured data (databases and data resources) and unstructured (content, document, records, and knowledge management).

Roles

In a *Command-and-Control* approach to data governance, management assigns employees new roles. Immediately, employees perceive data governance as something that is over and above their existing levels of responsibility, and thoughts turn to how much time it will take and how data governance competes with completing their job function.

In a *Traditional* approach to data governance, management identifies employee roles based on seniority and ownership of systems and data resources. Policy describes responsibilities requiring governance of formal charters and designation of people to play specific roles as part of the data governance program.

In a *Non-Invasive* approach to data governance, management recognizes employee roles based on their existing relationship to data. People who define data are guided through the data definition process when defining new data. People who produce data understand the impact of the data they produce. Data users are formally educated, made aware of, and expected to follow all rules associated with using data. Being recognized for something brings with it a positive connotation and positive expectations.

Process

In a *Command-and-Control* approach to data governance, all processes are new and governed. Data governance is all about taking control and redirecting processes specifically to govern the data. Management tells employees that data governance is why they follow the process, and it spells out penalties for not following it.

In a *Traditional* approach to data governance, there is a single process for governing data. Often, the process is labeled "The Data Governance Process." The process is applied to every activity and recognized as the main dimension of the program. By calling processes *data governance processes*, the discipline is singled out as the reason for having delays.

In a *Non-Invasive* approach to data governance, governance is applied to existing and new processes. We do not give processes the label of being a data governance process—they retain their original names, such as "request for access," "issue resolution," and "project methodology." When new processes are defined, they, too, are governed from the beginning.

Communications

In a *Command-and-Control* approach to data governance, data governance is communicated with a tone of "you will do this." Data governance is new to the people and the organization; and people are told exactly what to do in an authoritative manner. This is not always bad. In fact, some organizations require strong top-down direction and the demand for improved behavior.

In a *Traditional* approach to data governance, data governance is communicated as something that you should do. Oftentimes, data governance is spelled out in policy, and a directive is given for a specific group of people to take primary responsibility for governing data across the organization. This is also not always bad. For this approach to achieve results, people must be held accountable for doing what they are told.

In a *Non-Invasive* approach to data governance, data governance is communicated as something we already do but can do better. Since people are recognized for their relationship to the data, most responsibilities are conveyed through the formalization of activities that people already have associated with how they define, produce, and use data.

Metrics

In a *Command-and-Control* approach to data governance, the program's effectiveness is often measured in terms of Return on Investment (ROI). In other words, the expectation is that data governance will bring in money directly from the results of governing data through improved capabilities or through saving the organization money directly due to the governance of data. Unfortunately, these results are often difficult to demonstrate.

In a *Traditional* approach to data governance, the quality of data is used to measure the effectiveness of the program. Typically, organizations benchmark the quality of data definition, production, and usage, and put metrics in place to measure the improvement associated with the different domains of data quality, such as accuracy, completeness, timeliness, and relevance.

In a *Non-Invasive* approach to data governance, value is demonstrated from the return expected from investments the organization is making in data and analytical-based resources. Return on investment is typically measured from improved operational efficiency and effectiveness of analytical capabilities brought forth from other investments in information technology.

Tools

In a *Command-and-Control* approach to data governance, the early purchase of tools raises expectation levels. With this approach, the tool becomes the program's focus and people must learn the tool and integrate it into their daily routines and processes. Management often selects data governance tools without understanding tool capabilities and requirements.

In a *Traditional* approach to data governance, people leverage existing tools before new tools are acquired to enable data governance. Organizations following this approach look first to the tools they have in place and focus on specific activities such as improving data definition through modeling, data production through improved integration capabilities, and data usage through data protection capabilities.

In a *Non-Invasive* approach to data governance, people leverage existing tools and industry-proven templates and models to define requirements for future tool needs. The Non-Invasive approach calls for developing tools internally and leveraging existing industry templates that address specific governance needs to flush out detailed tool purchase requirements.

Each of the three different approaches can be effective.
And each comes with its upsides and downsides.

Key Messages

This essay summarized the three approaches to data governance and provided considerations for how each of the core components of a success data governance program are viewed in terms of the three approaches. Programs can follow different approaches for different components. This will be different from organization to organization.

Experience: What Makes a Data Element Critical?

There are always new terms appearing in the data world. While newfangled terms like "data mesh" and "data fabric" require lengthy descriptions, the term "critical data element" or CDE is easier to explain. As the name implies, CDEs are critical to data management, data governance, data quality, and the enterprise's success. Let's learn more about CDEs.

Before I get started, it is important to note that individual data elements are subsets of data resources that may house hundreds, if not thousands, of data elements. Best practice has demonstrated that organizations are better off focusing on subsets of data rather than trying to improve the quality and value of all the data at once.

When organizations take an incremental approach to implementing formal data disciplines, they must mature through experience and incrementally improve their management and governance techniques. Initial use cases for data governance, data management, and data quality programs should begin by focusing on selected CDEs. Then address additional CDEs using what you learned from the initial use case. Learn from experience and improve with each occurrence to cover an expanding amount of data critical to your organization.

Let's start by defining a data element and then tackle what it means to be critical. A data element is:

- *Any atomic unit of data defined for processing with a precise meaning.* In other words, databases, tables, and files (even spreadsheets and reports) have many pieces (units) of data. Each singular piece is considered a data element. For example, a customer address can be considered a singular data element or a collection of data elements—street, city, state, territory, country, and so on.

- *Defined by size (in characters) and type (alphanumeric, numeric only, true/false, date).* Every data element has specific characteristics representing how that data is stored in the data resource. For example, a country code may be a text field with a defined length that pulls its allowable values from a reference table of country codes. Only permitting selected codes from a reference table ensures the element is standard and consistent in length and value.

A data element is a singular piece of data. Just one. The most atomic unit of data there is. Examples include account number, Social Security Number, birth date, dollar amount, and so on. The truth is that many data elements may be considered critical to your organization. And different CDEs will be critical to different people.

There is no perfect answer to the question about how many data elements should be considered critical and included in each use case. Some organizations start with a very small number (three to five). Other organizations begin with a dozen (or dozens of) CDEs. Others even still have started down the path of focusing on CDEs numbering as many as fifty or more. Again, consider that there will always be more data elements.

It is important to note that each CDE is like an octopus. It has tentacles. CDEs rarely stand alone and are influenced by, and influence, other data elements. For example, an organization's pay grade may depend on a hire date that depends on the employee's status. Very few data elements stand alone. A proper number of CDEs to start will demonstrate value to the organization given the availability of time, resources, expectations, and required effort. Typically, grouping related data elements together when applying data disciplines makes sense. Grouped examples include mailing address elements (i.e., city, state, zip), person name elements (i.e., first name, middle initial, last name), or related elements that make up a specific transaction (like a sale or an event occurrence).

In many cases, the importance of data depends on who you ask. What is critical to one person, or even an entire department or division, may not be important or used by other people, departments, or divisions. People within a single part of the organization often access their data from different resources or use different data to complete their functions. There is no single definition of what data is critical to your organization. But given a standard criterion that assists you in focusing on important data first, not all your data will be considered critical.

Use these guidelines for determining if a piece of data is critical and, therefore, a CDE. Several items on this list were shared with me through client discussions, while others are general ideas for determining which data elements are CDEs. A data element may be identified as critical if the singular piece of data is:

- Noted as being critical or protected by organizational policy.
- Considered to be "connective tissue" between information systems.
- Considered to be the "grout between the tiles" or an element necessary to improve the meaning and usefulness of other pieces of data.
- Used as a key performance indicator (KPI) based on and substantiated by this element.
- Data that is key to the business.
- An element that helps the organization prioritize its work.
- Associated with regulatory fines/penalties or compliance violation risks.
- Associated with significant financial impact risk, such as increased liabilities, costs, or penalties, as well as a reduction in assets, revenue opportunities, or profits.
- Associated with interruption or significant reduction of critical business process risk, for an extended period.

Many organizations have documented a process to quantify the criticality of a data element. The process starts by determining the factors (like those listed above) for selecting CDEs.

Key Messages

Organizations are incrementally implementing data strategies by focusing their data governance, data management, and data quality initiatives on improving the value they get from their critical data. Since it is impossible to instantly have the same level of formal discipline associated for all of the data in the organization, it is important to have a method to prioritize the critical data that will be in focus. This essay focused on improving your definition of a critical data element.

Experience: A Data Governance Maturity Model

From time to time, organizations ask me to use a traditional Capability Maturity Model (CMM) to evaluate their data governance maturity. In this essay, I will align a known capability model with several aspects of data governance.

The following statement comes from Wikipedia, "The Capability Maturity Model, a registered service mark of Carnegie Mellon University (CMU), is a development model created after a study of data collected from organizations that contracted with the U.S. Department of Defense. This model became the foundation from which Carnegie Mellon created the Software Engineering Institute (SEI). The term 'maturity' relates to the degree of formality and optimization of processes, from ad hoc practices to formally defined steps, to managed result metrics, to active optimization of the processes."

"The term 'maturity' relates to the degree of formality and optimization of processes, from ad-hoc practices to formally defined steps, to managed result metrics, to active optimization of the processes."

When an organization applies the model to its existing software-development processes, it allows an effective approach to improving these processes. When an organization applies the model to its processes and structures of governing data, it can improve its processes and structures.

Over time it became clear that the model could also be applied to many other processes. This gave rise to a more general concept applied to many business areas. For example, many companies systematically planning their data governance evolution use data governance maturity models to control change by determining the appropriate level for their business and use of technology—and how and when to move from one level to the next. Each stage requires a certain investment, primarily in the use of internal resources. The rewards from a data governance program increase while risks decrease as the organization proceeds through each level.

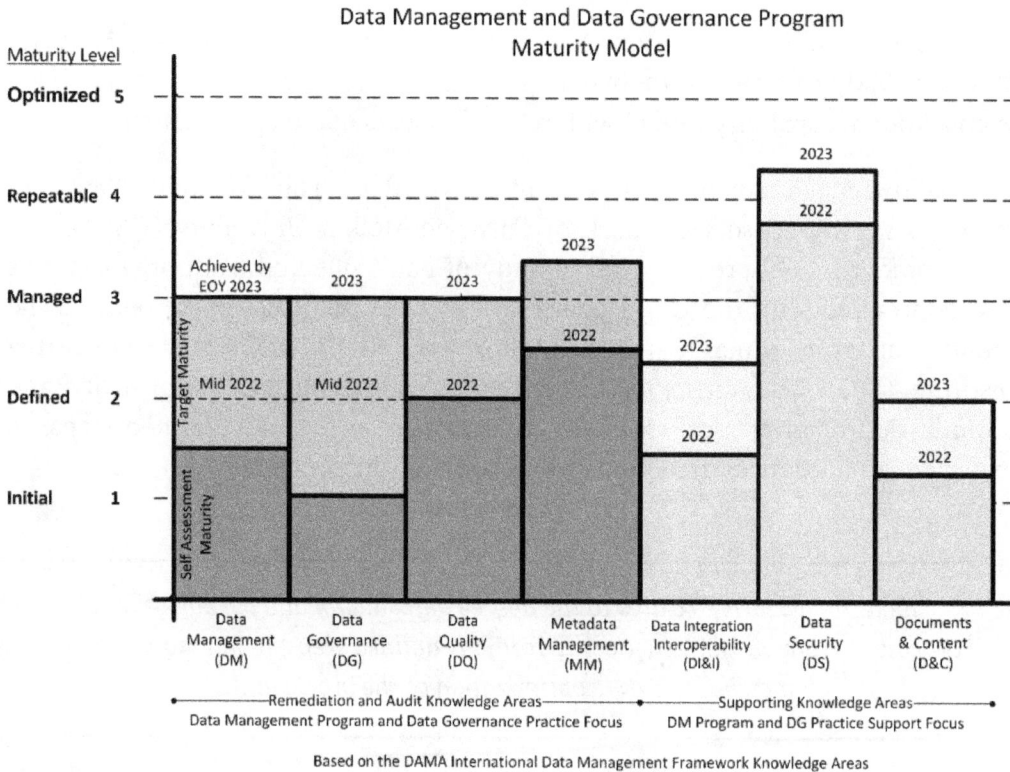

Data Management and Data Governance Program Maturity Model

Figure 1-5. Sample Data Management and Data Governance Maturity Model

Level 1—Initial Level

It is characteristic of processes at this level that they are typically undocumented and in a state of dynamic change, tending to be driven in an ad-hoc, uncontrolled, and reactive manner by users or events. This provides a chaotic or unstable environment for the processes. The Level 1 organization has no strict rules or procedures regarding data governance. Data may exist in multiple files and databases using multiple formats (known and unknown) and stored redundantly across multiple systems (by different names and using different data types). Few, if any, attempts have been made to catalog what exists.

Reports are developed "on the fly" as business units request them. The quality of data in a Level 1 organization depends on the skills of the technical IT analysts and developers. A level 1 organization will take on monumental tasks with little knowledge of their impact, causing project cancellations or, even worse, completed package implementations and updates with severely corrupted data and/or invalid reports. As a rough estimate, approximately 30% to 50% of organizations operate at Level 1.

Level 2—Defined Level

It is characteristic of processes at this level that there are sets of defined and documented standard processes established and subject to some degree of improvement over time. These standard processes are in place (i.e., they are the AS-IS processes) and are used to establish consistency of process performance across the organization. Organizations that successfully move from Level 2 to Level 3 on the data governance maturity scale have documented and established a data governance program as a core component of their report development and data usage life cycle. The program is enforced, and testing is done to ensure that data quality requirements are defined and met.

Level 2 organizations typically understand the business meaning of data and have created an organization-wide data governance function. Level 2 organizations have made the statement that "data is treated as a corporate asset," even if they do not entirely understand what that means. The success of the Level 2 organization typically depends on the interaction between the data governance and project management functions and the proper utilization of tools. Although Level 1 and Level 2 organizations may have tools at their disposal, they usually do not apply them consistently or correctly (sometimes they linger as "shelf-ware"). Tools are used by Level 2 organizations to record and maintain data governance documentation, and to automate data governance steps initiated to begin proactively monitoring and tuning data governance performance. Approximately 10% to 15% of organizations operate at Level 2.

Level 3—Managed Level

It is characteristic of processes at this level that, using process metrics, management can effectively control the AS-IS process (e.g., for software development). In particular, management can identify ways to adjust and adapt the process to particular projects without measurable losses of quality or deviations from specifications. Process Capability is established from this level.

An organization can move to Level 3 only when it institutes a managed metadata (data about data) environment. This enables the data governance team to catalog and maintain metadata for corporate data structures. It also provides the information technology and end-user staff access to what data exists within the organization (along with definitions, synonyms, homonyms, etc.). The data governance team is involved (at some level) in all development efforts to assist them in cataloging metadata and reducing redundant data elements (in logical models always and in physical models as appropriate for performance and project requirements). In addition, Level 3 organizations have begun to do data audits to gauge production data quality.

The success of the Level 3 organization depends on the buy-in of upper management to support the "data is a corporate asset" maxim. This involves treating data as they treat other assets (personnel, finances, buildings, finished goods, etc.). The organization uses advanced tools to manage metadata (repositories), data quality (transformation engines), and databases (agent-based monitors, centralized consoles for heterogeneous database administration, etc.).

Approximately 15% to 20% of organizations operate at Level 3. Upon successful implementation of a data governance launch and the ability to repeat these same steps for future data governance launch-like activities, the organization will be well on its way to becoming a Level 4 organization.

Level 4—Repeatable Level

It is characteristic of some processes at this level to be repeatable, possibly with consistent results. Process discipline is unlikely to be rigorous, but where it exists, it may help to ensure that the organization maintains existing processes during times of stress. To move from Level 1 to Level 2, an organization must begin to adhere to data governance best practices. To move to Level 3, the organization achieves consistent levels of achieving best practices. The best practices (typically) define four to six practices upon which the organization builds the data governance action plan.

Level 4 organizations follow a governance program that has become institutionalized to the point where the actions of governing data have become truly repeatable. These organizations often rely on a central person or group to understand the issues and implement data governance consistently. This has manifested itself in the creation of the well-established data governance team function.

The success of Level 4 organizations depends on the technical analysts' skills in managing the "technical" aspects of data. Although the differences between the business and technical aspects of data are usually (though not always) understood at some level, there is less effort to document and capture the business meaning of data. In addition, there is little (or no) differentiation between the logical and physical data design. Level 3 organizations will begin to institute data governance practices focused on a specific type of data used for Business Unit reporting. Moving from a Level 3 to a Level 4 organization requires becoming repeatable at improving the quality, value, and confidence in critical data associated with specific data resources. Approximately 5% to 10% of organizations operate at Level 4.

Level 5—Optimized Level

A characteristic of processes at this level is that the focus is on continually improving process performance through incremental and innovative technological changes/improvements.

The Level 5 organization uses the practices evolved in Levels 1 through 4 to continually improve data access, data quality, and database performance. Before introducing a production data store change, the data governance team scrutinizes and documents it within the metadata repository. Level 5 organizations are continually trying to improve the processes of data governance. Less than 5% of organizations operate at Level 5.

Key Messages

Figure 1-5 demonstrates how the levels described in this essay can be applied to the data governance and data management disciplines. Start by defining the levels of maturity that make sense to your organization. I have flipped CMU's CMM Levels 3 and 4 in the model I shared above because, in the data management and data governance disciplines, I find it hard to become repeatable before becoming managed. This is the beauty of creating your own data governance maturity model.

CHAPTER 2

Perspectives to Consider

Over the years, "problems with data" have been described many different ways. Many ways bring new perspectives to the issues associated with governing data that make the topic relatable to people who do not live and breathe data governance. Some of these ways are humorous, while others are memorable because they make a special connection through the language or concept that is used.

This chapter will most likely be fun to read. This chapter includes several short essays to extend your perception and understanding of data-related concepts through analogies. In addition, this chapter includes essays that challenge traditional ways of looking at data governance while making the subject of data governance easier to understand. I wrote these essays to advance the data-public's understanding of ways to look at data and data governance.

Perspective: Fix the "Data Situation"

What would you do with your data (i.e., what type of analytics would you run) if you had the data to support doing it and you had confidence in the quality of that data? What questions would you ask? What behavior would you predict? What relationships would you look for to gain business insights? These are all questions executives ask around the globe.

Management and analysts looking into the future find that they do not necessarily have the data they need to support these capabilities. This is becoming a big problem for organizations that believe they are leading the way in using information technology. They have data problems.

As leadership recognizes a data problem standing in their way of taking full advantage of their information technology investments, the door has opened wide to address what I will call the *data situation*. It sounds mysterious, but the truth is that it is not mysterious. Improving data quality to improve analytical capabilities can be the gateway to addressing larger data situations. Data practitioners should follow their leadership, looking to improve analytical capabilities to develop and apply a data strategy and data governance to their most critical data.

Allow me to share a handful of data situations:

- **Situation 1:** The data you use in your job is of decent quality. The data is there, but you must spend significant time massaging it to get it the way you like it.

- **Situation 2:** Data is missing. There are specific pieces of data that you focus on to evaluate performance, and it is a struggle to get that data or trust that data at its face value.

- **Situation 3:** You request data to complete your job and often have to jump through hoops to access that data. The process is slow. There are levels upon levels of approvers.

- **Situation 4**: Data from outside your "corporate" data is inconsistent from division to division. Some divisions provide high-quality data, while others scrap together spreadsheets to submit.

- **Situation 5**: People do not understand the difference between the data collected about a *school* loan versus the data collected about a *home* loan. You have single definitions of loan data, while the collected data is for a different context. You have limited or no glossaries or dictionaries to share the appropriate data meaning at the appropriate time.

Data situations stink. Any one of these sample situations can lead to making the wrong decision, causing a costly business impact, leaving sensitive data unprotected, or losing ground with your closest competitors. As a result, we all want to address the data situation.

Here are three things that you can do right now to address a bad data situation:

1. *Realize that your data can be better.* There are several ways to do this. Often the efforts focus on the people of your organization. How do they feel about the data situation they deal with daily? Where do they spend their time? Do they trust the data, or better yet, why don't they trust the data? Do they understand the data, and do they know where to go to get the data they need? How would they answer the questions at the beginning of this section? The answers to these questions can be viewed as the impending key to Pandora's Box or the key to the Magic Kingdom. Regardless of whether you focus on customer data and the customer experience, product data and the definition of product, or on classification and protection of sensitive data—realize that there is room for improvement regarding your data situation.

2. *Identify a person or persons that will have time allocated to focus on correcting the data situation.* This person or team should be responsible for researching, inventorying, cataloging, assessing, measuring, and maturing the data environment. Ideally, there are two people: one responsible for ensuring the data situation improves and one responsible for the activities mentioned in this section. The truth is that without someone accountable and responsible for the data strategy or data

governance, the discipline will fail. That, of course, holds true for any discipline you are trying to apply, not just data management. In many organizations, the accountable person is at a higher organizational management level than the responsible person.

3. The third thing you can do is *build an immaculate business case for the need to improve data and information across your organization.* There may already be somebody responsible for this activity. You may not know them yet. But likely, somewhere in your halls is a person or people who want to build a business case for governing and improving your data situation. Search them out. Share your story and drive the effort to build that business case. Leadership must demonstrate that the value of data goes beyond the nice-to-have when it comes to daily operations and business decision-making. The business case must demonstrate the present data situation compared to industry best practice, the gap and risk associated with that gap, and the steps to install a formal data strategy and data governance program. Then, and only then, you can show them the true business case and the effort required to improve the data situation.

Key Messages

Executives are finding that they do not have the data they need to support the new capabilities of the expanding data analytics space. Data has become a big problem for organizations that believe they are leading the way in using information technology. You can fix this situation.

Perspective: Data Governance as a Puzzle

I debated whether to title this essay *Data Governance as a Puzzle* or *Data Governance is a Puzzle*. Both titles seem to make good sense.

I selected the first option and decided to use this essay to compare data governance and good puzzles rather than describe the puzzle. Oxford Dictionary defines a puzzle as "a problem designed to test ingenuity or knowledge."

Recently, I came across a light-hearted article written by Eleanor Robinson, founder of the gaming company 7-128, that outlined the characteristics of a good puzzle.[1] Her essay got me thinking about the similarities between data governance and a "good" puzzle. Therefore, I will use Robinson's characteristics of a good puzzle to lay out data governance as a puzzle.

Robinson started her essay by focusing on the characteristics of puzzle games that she plays often versus the characteristics of puzzles that she plays only a few times or never returns to play. This is a great analogy for data governance as most organizations want their stewards to continue playing (governing data) rather than leaving and never returning.

Many of the characteristics she defined apply directly to the success of data governance, while others may require a stretch of the imagination (or lengthy practical experience) to draw the comparison.

These are her characteristics of a good puzzle:

Re-Playability

Good puzzle characteristic: Game must have re-playability. (Robinson)

Data governance must be re-playable, or should I say, the actions of governing data must be repeatable. The data must serve multiple purposes (and thus be

---

[1] https://7128.com/.

reusable). The roles must be reusable, governed processes must be repeatable, communications consistent and repeatable, metrics and tools re-playable as well. In fact, just like in a puzzle, organizations improve the value, efficiency, and effectiveness of their governance activities through repetition.

Verdict: Based on this characteristic, data governance is a puzzle.

Engagement

Good puzzle characteristic: The puzzle must be engaging enough that you lose track of time and what else is happening around you for at least brief periods when you are playing it. (Robinson)

One statement I keep making about data governance is that activating data stewards is the only way to implement an effective program. I have said, "everybody is a data steward," and organizations must find a way to get past that fact and deal with it to provide coverage to the entire organization. Data governance programs that demonstrate success to their organizations activate and engage their data stewards, help the stewards to recognize themselves as data stewards, and engage data stewards where they "touch" the data. Just like in a puzzle, finding the most effective way to engage is to utilize data stewards to test ingenuity to solve problems and address opportunities.

Verdict: A key characteristic of a good puzzle is how the puzzle engages you. A key characteristic of a data governance program is how you will engage the stewards and the rest of the organization. Data governance sounds like a good puzzle to me.

Requires Strategic Planning

Good puzzle characteristic: The puzzle must include some capability to do strategic planning, to plan ahead, and modify the outcome. Pure chance games lose their luster rapidly, no matter how pretty they are. (Robinson)

A plan for your data governance effort assures that your activities focus on achieving your target state. Instead of taking a "ready, fire, aim" approach where you shoot before you know your target, I always suggest aiming the data governance program at specific targeted activities. Often, we determine the target activities through an assessment or analysis against industry best practices for standing up a formal data governance program. Superior data governance plans are often agile, focusing on being efficient, effective, and able to modify the outcome of your program based on demonstrated success (or lack thereof). In addition, the ability to focus (and refocus) your data governance program based on planning ahead better prepares the program to react when the data governance puzzle gets complicated or threatened.

Verdict: Although a good puzzle provides some capability to do strategic planning, data governance requires the ability to plan and adjust to modify the outcome of your program. This puzzle characteristic aligns with data governance from the perspective that both require advanced planning and the ability to adjust actions to improve outcomes.

Time Factor

Good puzzle characteristic: There must be a time factor, either as a countdown clock or as a reward for faster play. Time must be adjustable for different skills, play modes, or ability levels. (Robinson)

Data governance programs are not typically time-based. However, program leaders do not have infinite time to demonstrate value to their organization or leadership. The value from a data governance program comes from improvements in data definition, production, and usage that require planning, execution, and measurement. Organizations often measure program success in two ways. The first way focuses on measuring the business value that comes from improved governance of data. This method of measuring program success takes time and requires that you record the present state for measuring change. The second way measures how well, or the rate at which the enterprise accepts and adopts the program. The second way results in measurements that can show governance improvements in a shorter period. The clock is always ticking. Plan to demonstrate success quickly and often to appease management's focus on the time factor. The next characteristic focuses on improvement through repetition. Repetition leads to improved skills and entrance into different data governance puzzle play modes (based on the organization's maturity level).

Verdict: The good puzzle characteristic of the time factor impacts every data governance program when demonstrable success must come quickly. Hopefully you will not reach the end of the time factor (5-4-3-2-1-done) before providing demonstrable reward to your organization.

Improvement Through Repetition

Good puzzle characteristic: Increase in skills through repetition should achieve higher scores, reach higher levels, and solve more difficult puzzles. This means it should not be solvable on the first try, but improving skill, not chance, should result in increased success. (Robinson)

Maturity comes through experience. Many published maturity models lay out a progression from an initial level of maturity to a defined level, then a repetitive level, before becoming managed and ultimately optimized. Organizations that plan for data governance success learn from their experience and improve how they govern data. When solving a good puzzle, players improve their ability through the experience of advancements and setbacks they experience when attempting to solve the puzzle. Data governance too, we learn by doing. Organizations mature at governing data over time. The holy grail of data governance is optimization, though, just like being able to solve a puzzle is the ultimate result.

Verdict: Data governance programs are good puzzles because organizations show improvement through repetition. Measurable success does not always come quickly, but organizations can learn from experience and improve simultaneously.

Easy Early Success

Good puzzle characteristic: You must have some success on the first try. This means it must be easy enough for everyone to achieve at least the first several screens (goals) at the easiest setting. (Robinson)

"Reach for low-hanging fruit" means that organizations should look to address opportunities that provide value quickly and without the most complex level of execution. Low hanging fruit means success in something that adds true value to the business without a prolonged period of execution. Data governance programs that demonstrate success early are given additional chances to continue demonstrating success. Shoot for the streetlights before you shoot for the stars. The streetlights are within reach on the first try, while reaching the stars requires planning, execution, and measurement— success will not come quickly.

Verdict: According to this characteristic, data governance is definitely a good puzzle. Success must come with some challenges, although the demonstration of early success entices organizations to keep working on the puzzle.

Definable Levels of Success

Good puzzle characteristic: If it has levels, it should have variability between levels to add interest. Just making it faster or increasing numbers is NOT enough. This may include changing playing fields and rules of play or adding new hazards and graphic types. (Robinson)

As mentioned earlier, there are maturity levels that organizations use to define their success in data governance. After starting at the initial level, organizations move to the defined level, where they record and formalize the components of their program. Organizations achieve a repeatable level of success when the defined components are successful. Organizations achieve the managed level when the repeatable actions they take demonstrate value. An organization reaches the optimized pinnacle level by constantly improving their data governance score. These defined levels of success are used widely when organizations conduct data governance readiness assessments.

Verdict: Data governance is a good puzzle according to this characteristic because organizations that focus on continuous improvement often get better at demonstrating levels of success over time.

Ability to Break through Barriers

Good puzzle characteristic: If chance locks out the possibility of a solution, there should be something—a bonus gained previously or some item of value that can break through the lock-out at least sometimes. Otherwise, it becomes boring if you always fail at a particular level or pattern. Using a "bomb" is an example of such an item of value. But these objects should not be too [easily] available or it will become boring if you can always have something to use to win the game. You need to fail occasionally. (Robinson)

This characteristic only applies slightly to assess whether or not data governance is a good puzzle. Data governance programs reach obstacles and barriers to success all the time. Whether it is a change in leadership, a change in resources, a change in organizational focus, or any other change to the organization, the resources of a data governance program are typically impacted. These barriers to success can be considered puzzle roadblocks or things that cause you to take a step back and re-evaluate your approach to solve the puzzle or implement your data governance program. Barriers are common. Some people may even say that foreseeing the barriers of success and tackling those problems early make the life of a data governance program administrator (puzzle solver) an exciting challenge.

Verdict: Data governance programs, like good puzzles, always face barriers. Successful program leaders successfully address those barriers, continuously making their program-oriented efforts "interesting" and challenging.

Components and the Approach

Good puzzle characteristic: A large variety of different piece arrangements should occur randomly when you start the game. The same setup should not always appear. One factor that makes a game of cards so appealing is that, basically, no two layouts or hands are the same. (Robinson)

My data governance framework shared in an earlier essay has been enhanced over time. The framework consists of six core components (data, roles, processes, communications, metrics, and tools) viewed from five organizational levels (executive, strategic, tactical, operational, and support) to demonstrate all the pieces of an effective data governance program. I consider these to be the pieces of the complete data governance puzzle. Organizations typically do not focus on the entire framework at one time. Instead, they work on a specific component or two, or a specific level or two, to improve by learning from experience and improving in their maturity before they move on and attempt to tackle the next component. Combining all the pieces (components) over time increases your chance of solving the puzzle (demonstrating data governance program success) dramatically.

Verdict: Data governance is a puzzle according to this characteristic because it has several components that can be improved through experience and completed incrementally.

Key Messages

In this essay, I have compared data governance to the characteristics of a good puzzle. I debated writing about the puzzling and challenging aspects of data governance (of which there are many) but decided instead to write about how data governance and puzzles share features. There are many characteristics of good puzzles that are also characteristics of effective data governance programs. I hope comparing puzzles and data governance makes sense when considering the work necessary to implement data governance.

Data governance is just like a puzzle. Enjoy solving data governance!

Perspective: Data is Like Contaminated Water

What if the water flowing through your house or apartment pipes was contaminated, and you knew drinking or bathing in this water would make you sick? Like most home dwellers, you would invest in putting water filters everywhere to reduce contamination exposure.

What if you owned a one-hundred-unit apartment building, and the water was bad for all tenants? It is costlier to install one hundred water filters to cover your liability. Instead, you may start thinking about putting a water filtration system in the place where the water enters the property. This would take care of the problem once and for all and allow you to maintain consistent water quality for everyone in your building. This larger solution may cost a bit more, but it would greatly reduce risk, improve customer satisfaction, and save you money in the long run.

Shhh. Don't tell anybody, but your data may be contaminated. It may be incomplete, inaccurate, untimely, un-integrate able, and/or unprotected. Ask the people that define, produce, and use data in your organization if your data is safe. That is, formally defined, produced, and used across the organization. Then ask them how the data could be better. If your management knew the truth about the water...I mean the data problems; do you think they'd drink from that source? Most likely not. It makes sense that they would want to remedy the situation.

Your data is just like the water flowing through your personal pipes or into many people's homes and functions in your organization. The data feeds and flows from your processes, decision-making, and, ultimately, your organization's people. Data problems stem from poorly designed data resources, system and organization acquisitions, silos, and individualized investments made in data warehousing, business intelligence, big data, smart data, and metadata applications—all investments of your organization's hard-earned dollars. Your organization can choose to clean up the data problem whenever it rears its ugly head, like in the individual apartment unit example, or you can put a data governance program in place to improve the quality, usefulness, and protection of the data systematically and consistently.

Data governance is the execution and enforcement of authority
over the management of data and data-related assets.
In simpler terms, data governance requires formal accountability for data.

I suggest that organizations follow the Non-Invasive Data Governance approach. The term "non-invasive" describes how to exercise data governance: people's roles are formalized based on their relationship with the data, and we apply governance to existing processes and functions. This approach is the most practical and effective approach being shared today. It is easier, but not necessarily easy.

Let's go back to your home for a moment. Putting a water filter on your kitchen sink does not improve the drinkability of the water in the bathroom. Likewise, the filter in the fridge does not improve water quality in the bathtub. One-off solutions do not fix the overall problem.

The data quality tool used to clean data as it enters the data warehouse does not solve the data quality issues at the sourcing systems. Protecting who can see the data in one application does not prevent the wrong people from seeing the data in another application. Focusing on cleaning up the contaminated data on a systematic scale is the only long-term solution.

Key Messages

Moving forward with a formalized Non-Invasive Data Governance program requires that somebody at a higher level in your organization recognizes that your data is contaminated. Some senior leadership will get it, but some won't. If you are in an organization that does not value the need to formally govern data, maybe this anecdote about comparing contaminated water to dirty data will help them to get the message.

Perspective: Data Anarchy Versus Governance

Are we in an age of data anarchy? When we look at all the data we use in our personal and business lives, it is scary to think that most of this data is ungoverned and in a state of data anarchy.

Anarchy is defined in several ways, but there is a theme to all the definitions. Anarchy is a state of disorder due to absence or nonrecognition of authority.[2] Anarchy is the condition of a society, entity, group of people, or a single person that rejects hierarchy.[3] Anarchy is the type of government where there is no government at all. Every person is left to fight for themselves.[4]

If anarchy is a lack of government, that translates to a lack of governance. If there is a lack of governance of the data we consume daily, both in our business and personal lives, does that mean that we live in the age of data anarchy?

Data Anarchy in Our Daily Lives

Think about the large amount of data you produce and use daily. Whether it is data you create with every keystroke or click of the mouse, the data you create when you use your credit or debit card, or the data created when you use your phone, move your car down the highway, or watch the television. You are creating data about yourself at every turn. The management of that data is often in a state of disorder due to an absence of integrated authority for handling that data. That is data anarchy.

Most of us don't think about the anarchy or lack of formal governance around the personal data we produce all day. We don't worry about it because the

---

[2] Google definition.

[3] "Decentralism: Where It Came From-Where Is It Going?" Amazon.com.

[4] WOU.edu definition.

governance of that data is hidden from the average person. Unfortunately, the more we learn about mishandling some of our data, the more nervous we get.

It is easiest to rest assured that highly paid people in these organizations are responsible for moving their organizations from data anarchy to a governed environment.

Now let's look at our business life. Is the data environment at our organizations being handled like a data anarchy or as a governed environment? What does business data anarchy look like versus a governed business data environment?

Business Data Anarchy Versus Governed Data

How can you tell if the data in your organization is in a state of data anarchy or resembles a governed data environment?

Data anarchies typically have these characteristics:

- There is no formal accountability for the definition, production, and use of data.

- No one is responsible for overseeing data subject matters as a cross-business asset.

- There is no formal process for escalating data issues to a strategic level that makes decisions.

- There are irresponsible investments and management of high-profile data-related projects.

- There are inefficient/ineffective processes associated with leveraging data for decision-making.

- People that handle data are uncertain of the rules associated with sensitive data.

A governed data environment has these characteristics:

- People that define, produce, and use data are formally accountable for following the documented and communicated rules associated with defining, producing, and using that data.

- Some people are responsible for managing data across business areas, business functions, and major data integration projects.

- There is formal accountability for following an agreed-upon process to escalate data issues to the appropriate level of the organization.

- Investments and high-profile data integration projects are strongly vetted with an intent focus on the organization's data requirements.

- Business and technical processes associated with managing data are formalized, and people are held accountable for following the processes.

- People handling the data are well-versed and audited in following the rules for protecting sensitive data.

Are We Really Living in a Business Data Anarchy?

Most organizations know they have problems associated with their data. The problems may be with the quality of the data, how the data is protected, and regulatory and compliance concerns. The problems may be with what it takes you to access the data and analyze it to make the best possible and real-time decisions.

These same organizations are investing millions of dollars in huge data-oriented projects where data requirements may or may not be integral to their Agile software development or integrated data delivery efforts. They may have grown through acquisition and may have several supply chain, human resource, or finance functions attempting to synchronize and update their processes.

Is it appropriate to call these environments data anarchies? Well, no and yes. No because it takes time and a formal effort to gain support, sponsorship, and understanding at the highest level and to formalize and deploy a data governance effort across an organization. Yes, it most likely is a data anarchy—an ungoverned mess. So, what are you waiting for if your organization has not started moving from anarchy to governance?

Key Messages

Data governance is "the execution and enforcement of authority over managing data and data-related resources." Anarchy is defined as no governance at all. Therefore, organizations that cannot execute and enforce authority over the management of data definition, production, and usage are most likely in an anarchy state.

The Sex Pistols, a classic punk band in a classic punk-era, articulated anarchy in their song "Anarchy in the U.K."—included in the Rock and Roll Hall of Fame's 500 Songs that Shaped Rock and Roll.[5] "I don't know what I want. I know how to get it." The truth is that many organizations know what they want, but don't know how to get it. Therefore, organizations must move from data anarchy to data governance if they want to get the most value out of their data.

---

[5] "500 Songs That Shaped Rock." Rock and Roll Hall of Fame.

Perspective: Defeat Your Data Demons

Stories you read in the news occasionally mention how a person battles their demons: alcoholism, drug addiction, and compulsive behaviors like gambling. Demons take many forms. The word "demon" immediately tilts the context toward something that is not good. There are times when demons rule the day.

Organizations have demons too.

Just like people, some organizations are battling their known demons, while some know they have demons yet do not attempt to address them. Organizational demons may be politically based, culturally, gender, ignorance, or even data-based. Organization's data demons are real.

I define data demons as data-related behaviors that we know are wrong yet we continue to follow the ill-advised way of acting. Many organizations work to improve these demons daily while others have difficulty acknowledging that they have demons. Let's look at the forms these data demons take, and how to address them.

Data Demons generally take three forms:

- Data Definition Demons
- Data Production Demons
- Data Usage Demons

Data Definition Demons

Let's start where data is defined. Data definition takes place through data modeling exercises, software package implementation, application development, the incorporation of external data sources, and by defining data in new databases and information systems.

Data should be well-defined at the beginning of its lifecycle so that it is well-understood throughout that lifecycle. Sufficient data definition requires thorough collection and development of data requirements, which is one area where organizations have data demons. Taking the time to collect business data requirements and develop sound business definitions for data has not always been the focus of traditional information system development methods. Agile development efforts have further complicated matters by requiring quick and incremental delivery of complex information systems, leaving little time to flush out data problems while accumulating data debt.

Data governance can battle data definition demons in many ways. My definition of data governance shared earlier in the book calls for the "execution and enforcement of authority over data," meaning that authority must be used to make certain that data is defined in such a way that it will assist the organization in getting the most out of that data. Data governance can battle data definition demons by formalizing the involvement of the "right" people at the "right" time in the data definition process and by getting the "right" people to authorize that a data definition is thorough and complete.

Data definition includes a focus on metadata, including business descriptions, standardized naming of the data, data lineage and location, business rules, and compliance and handling rules—whatever the organization determines is important to squeeze maximum value out of their data.

Data definition demons become evident when the data definition is not complete or shared with the business users of that data. If business people do not understand the data, know where they can find the "right" data, and don't know how they can use the data, data definition demons are present.

Data Production Demons

We produce data to meet business needs. Unfortunately, the production of data can have demons too. Data production demons become evident when the people and process responsible for producing data do not understand why the data is collected, how the data must be produced, or how it will be used. Cashiers entering the store's postal code rather than the customer's postal code, office staff reordering patient diagnosis codes, accepting default data rather than entering correct data, and sharing data that is supposed to be held private, are all results of people not being held accountable for how they produce data.

Data production demons are the result of an inability to communicate effectively with your data production stewards (people that are held accountable for producing data) regarding how the data must "look" when it is entered or transferred, the inability to prevent bad data from getting into the systems, or the poor timing or quality of required data sources.

Data production demons may result from laziness or allowing a customer to be added to the central customer database a second, third, or tenth time (spelled or abbreviated slightly different). This same demon may appear because the customer information is housed in numerous unsynchronized data stores. This same demon may appear for vendors, doctors, patients, or whoever is the customer of your business.

Data production demons are often a result of data definition demons—where data is not defined completely or accurately, making it impossible for quality data production. Data governance can battle data production demons by getting the "right" people involved at the "right" time with the "right" understanding and "right" limitations (or edits) to produce quality data. Remember my definition of data governance and that authority over data production must be enforced to ensure the organization gets the most out of its data.

Data Usage Demons

Data usage demons may be the most prevalent demons in organizations. Data usage demons result from improper or ineffective use of data for many reasons: lack of understanding, lack of access, lack of knowing the handling rules, lack of consistency and quality, and so on.

Data definition and data production demons result in poor data quality, making it difficult to improve the effective use of data. Executives want dashboards that provide consistent answers when they ask critically important questions and make enterprise-level decisions. People at the strategic and tactical levels of the organization want to use data to research and develop great products, services, and enhance customer relationships. People at the operational level need to use data to perform their daily responsibilities.

Data usage demons become evident whenever someone says, "just give me all of the data and then I will tell you what data I need," or they use data they don't fully understand. Data usage demons result in grueling processes associated with pulling data together for any purpose, including customer reporting, government or industry reporting, or responding to an executive's request for numbers.

Data governance can battle data usage demons in many ways. The execution and enforcement of authority over data definition, production, and usage must be applied to use data efficiently and effectively, protect sensitive data, share data appropriately, and become a data-centric organization. All of these demons require improved communications and awareness about the data that is being governed.

Key Messages

Data demons prevent the organization from being all it can be. You may recognize that your organization has only a few data demons, or maybe it has many. If you let the demons fester, you can expect things to stay the same—reporting and decision-making will not improve, data inefficiency and ineffectiveness will continue to be a liability, and the people of your organization will become demons themselves as they find their own way to solve data matters because of a lack of formal governance.

Implement an effective data governance program to battle your data demons. Data governance is the only way to apply formal accountability for data, execute and enforce authority for data, and deal with our beasts, ogres, and behemoths.

Perspective: Your Organization Has the Data Flu

Is your organization feeling any pain or suffering from poor quality, lack of protection, or modest understanding of your data? The chances are that your organization is feeling the pain. The germs are all around you, the symptoms are obvious, and the treatment or cure may or may not be readily available. Your organization has the Data Flu.

I know that the treatments include a healthy dose of data governance.

The Germs

The germs of an unhealthy data environment come from the people, processes, and technologies associated with the data. People must do the "right" things when it comes to your organization's data. Specific people must have formal accountability to define data in ways that will be most beneficial to the business meaning, that forethought, strategic by nature, must be given to the definition of the data. If you don't have people responsible for strategic forethought of data definition, then germs are bound to multiply. It doesn't matter how much "data sanitizer" you use.

People must have a formal responsibility to produce the data such that it can be used as a strategic asset and fit for purposeful use. People must have formal responsibility for using the data the way it is intended to be used. This includes protecting sensitive data and conforming to the rules and regulations set forth by their industry and involved governments (where they service customers and partners). Without formal responsibility for the data, the data can become sick very quickly.

Without formal responsibility for the data,
the data can become sick very quickly.

Germs can come from any process that is not well defined or executed formally or effectively. Process often requires involving the *right* people at the *right* time and getting them to do the *right* things when it comes to defining, producing, and using data. In the first book, I referred to this as the Bill of "Rights." The Bill of "Rights" lies at the core of effective data governance.

The Symptoms

How are you supposed to recognize the symptoms of the data flu? Symptoms of ill data include data you do not trust, data you spend too much time manipulating before you can use it, data that is hard to get, or data that "you know you can trust" from only your reliable sources. Any or all those symptoms require attention. And the thing is, you probably already knew that. The problem in many cases is that no one in the organization is responsible for fixing what ails you.

This problem is like not having any doctors. Your organization has the symptoms, but you do not have anyone that will help you solve these problems. That is...until now. The people responsible for data governance are typically the symptom-solvers when recording, communicating, and gaining awareness at the appropriate level of the organization.

The Treatment and the Cure

Treatment for the data flu may not be simple and often only addresses a limited number of the symptoms. It is like the availability of a flu vaccine. The vaccine is available, but sometimes it can be only partially effective.

One of the first treatments I recommend is that the organization create the function of data governance and give someone the "Doctor of Data" responsibility. Perhaps your organization already has this function. The data governance function may exist under the Chief Data Officer (CDO) or Chief Data and Analytics Officer (CDAO), who could be considered the Chief Data Doctor in this essay. Gartner Group told us that 90% of large organizations would have a CDO by the year 2019.[6] 2019 is in the past and that expectation was not achieved.

If you do not have a chief data officer and the data governance function is not a part of the Chief Information Officer's responsibilities, look for the person with responsibility for improving analytical capabilities or with the term *data science* associated with their group. These are all good people to ask. And they are good people to get involved with if you are suffering from data flu symptoms.

The data governance function is about executing and enforcing authority over managing data and data-related assets. This function does not naturally happen without the formal responsibility to make it happen.

There are three approaches to building a formal data governance function that will be part of the healthy regiment used to address the data flu. A command-and-control approach requires the organization to assign people to roles they don't already play and feels over-and-above people's existing work effort. A traditional approach echoes "if you build the data governance function, they will come" and expects people to gravitate toward data governance. And finally, there is the non-invasive approach to data governance that assumes that people already have relationships to data that can be formalized in a way that doesn't feel invasive.

Key Messages

When you do not feel well or have the flu, the recommendation is to stay home and take care of yourself. You may even call the doctor. That's always a good idea. When your data is not well, you should do something about that too. Staying at home will not solve the problem.

The data governance function is one way organizations address their data flu problem. The data governance function needs to exist if your organization's data is going to get healthier.

---

[6] https://www.gartner.com/newsroom/id/3190117.

Perspective: The Four Horsemen of the Data Apocalypse

While I was attending a recent conference, one of the presenters spoke very briefly about the four horsemen of the data apocalypse.[7] The original four horsemen of the apocalypse are described in the last book of the New Testament as death, famine, war, and conquest as a symbolic prophecy of the future.

There are also four horsemen of the Data Apocalypse. The messages of the four horsemen of the data apocalypse focused on attitudes toward data, including ignorance, arrogance, obsolescence, and power, clearly describing why organizations struggle to manage their data as a valued asset.

Ignorance

The first horseman is Ignorance. The ignorance attitude is thinking that seeking value from data is not that important. Organizations that carry ignorance toward data attitude are at the lowest end of the data maturity spectrum. Organizations that demonstrate ignorance toward data are behind their competition when allocating resources focused on improving their data situation. Improvements in the data situation can include improving data quality, understanding, protection, and regulatory and compliance reporting capabilities. These organizations will be the last to hire Chief Data Officers (CDOs), implement formal data governance programs, and collect and manage the information about their data.

You have heard the statement that "ignorance is bliss." Well, not in this case. In this case, ignorance leads organizations to fall behind during the blossoming information age.

---

[7] Michael Atkins of the EDM Council.

Arrogance

The second horseman is Arrogance. The arrogance attitude is management thinking that they know more about the data than the people that are accountable for the data.

Organizations that maintain this attitude demonstrate the belief that management knows best. Management will not know their team's difficulties if they do not converse with those who know the data best. Avoid arrogance through open dialogue with the people who define, produce, and use data as part of their daily routine. Arrogance toward data can be avoided by conducting internal assessments of how the organization governs its data compared to industry best practices.

I read that unnamed philosophers speculate, "The difference between arrogance and confidence is performance."[8] Management should look at the data they use to improve their organization's performance and be open-minded toward continuous data governance and management.

Obsolescence

The third horseman is Obsolescence. The obsolescence attitude is thinking that the present data, in the present systems, will never die and that if it carried the organization this far, there is no reason to change.

Organizations with this attitude are afraid to move out of the past and invest in the future. To stay one step ahead of the competition, organizations must continuously focus on improving data quality, access, understanding, and protection, even if the present state allows the organization to get by. Organizations with obsolete data and systems become inefficient, ineffective, and act very informally toward improving their data situation.

---

[8] https://www.coachhub.com/blog/confidence-and-arrogance/.

As Andy Rooney, noted American radio and television personality, once said, "The fastest thing computers do is go obsolete."[9] The same can be said about data housed on these computers, and the systems that manage the flow and use of data on these computers. Resting on your data laurels is the quickest way to become obsolete.

Power

The last horseman is Power. The power attitude is the feeling that projects owned by the most influential members of management are more critical than other projects.

Organizations in which power is the driving attitude have a difficult time getting out of their own way when prioritizing those activities that will lead to higher-quality data. Power may come from having the most seniority or being associated with the most profitable part of the business. This power often is in the hands of people who see investments in their own personal data infrastructure as most important. While these projects are important, with limited resources, the most critical data needs of the organization are often misunderstood or misinterpreted as being less important.

William Gaddis, a famous American author, once said that "Power doesn't corrupt people, people corrupt power."[10] The truth is that the most powerful people in the organization must have the responsibility to know and understand the need to prioritize projects that will have the most valuable impact on the organization. Power moves often lead to bad decision-making, leading to the squeakiest wheels getting the grease while the other wheels fall off the axle.

---

9   http://img.picturequotes.com/2/492/491460/the-fastest-thing-computers-do-is-go-obsolete-quote-1.jpg.

10 https://www.forbes.com/quotes/9896/.

Key Messages

The four horsemen of the data apocalypse are a simplified way of looking at the impediments to an organization's ability to improve their data situation. The better we recognize these attitudes in our organization, the quicker and more effective we will be at addressing and managing the most important and valuable asset we own: our data.

Perspective: Time for a Data Intervention

Interventions are a systematic assessment and planning process employed to remediate or prevent a problem. The process often focuses on resolving social, educational, and developmental issues by bringing together friends, family, and people with the addressee's best interests. The intervention is often considered a last resort, or way to solve a problem, when all else has failed.

Has your organization reached the point where you require a data intervention with your data problems? You may know that your organization has a data problem. You may have even taken small steps over time or tried things, in different parts of your organization for specific types of data, in an attempt to solve the data problems.

But you know that the undercurrent of poor data management practices is so substandard or pervasive that it will require gathering people with your organization's best interest to solve this problem. There is a solution.

Don't wait until you have hit rock bottom. The opportunity is now to solve the data problem. How should you get started?

Start by asking:
Is it time for a data intervention?

Let's briefly go back to the definition at the beginning of this essay. If an intervention is a systematic process of assessment and planning, here are steps you can take to perform this type of activity:[11]

---

[11] Adapted from "How to Perform an Intervention" on wikiHow to do anything ... wikiHow.com.

Consult With a Professional

Seeking professional help is always a large part of interventions. The professionals can come from outside the group of people involved in the intervention, or inside the group if they know how to solve the problem.

The same can be said for organizations that either 1) have an internal person with the expertise to drive solutions or 2) need to look to the outside for professional help. This recognition that your organization has a problem and that you do not have the skills or experience to solve the problem yourself are logical first steps of an intervention.

Think about this in terms of data. Many data and information management professionals have the experience and know-how to assist you with your data issues as you adopt data-centric technologies associated with data analytics and artificial intelligence. If this person is not inside your organization, you should look to the outside.

Form an Intervention Team

What would an intervention team look like when it comes to improving your organization's data and information? Let's start with the person or persons that will be responsible for leading the team—because without a leader, teams tend to lose their sense of direction. A typical person in the role of Data Intervention Team Leader could be the Chief Officer associated with data (CDO), data and analytics (CDAO), information technology (CIO), or potentially risk (CRO).

Suppose that the chief person does not have the hands-on experience to lead the effort. In that case, they should still be recognized as being accountable for improving the data situation and select a person(s) that will be responsible (to them) for leading the effort. Other data intervention team members can include people responsible for data governance, management, architecture, analytics, and strategy. In addition, business representatives who are knowledgeable about the distributed data landscape and passionate about improving data value efficiency and effectiveness should also be on the team.

The discipline of data governance will be instrumental to the success of the data intervention team. I define data governance as the execution and enforcement of authority over data management because we must follow formal processes and rules to improve an organization's data situation.

Find the Right Treatment Plan

Speaking of data governance, selecting the appropriate approach to data governance is one of the best-determining factors of what it will take to deliver and sustain high-quality data and information for your organization. Therefore, select the approach that best fits the organizational culture and willingness to change in terms of how your organization manages their data. There are three approaches to data governance that are described in the Comparing Approaches to Data Governance essay in Chapter 1.

Regardless of your approach, people must be held formally accountable for the data they define. Then people that produce the data must be held accountable for the data they produce according to how the data is defined. Last, those that use the data must be held accountable for how they use the data. There are non-threatening treatment plans available through education and training to get people to improve their existing relationships with the data. With this approach, "you are already doing this," which certainly has a non-invasive appeal.

Decide on Consequences to Put Forward

In an intervention, people focus on the consequences of continuing to behave in a specific way. They focus on how the behavior impacts people and on what to do to solve the problem. An early step in an intervention is to spell out the consequences of the bad behavior. This relates directly to the common data and information problems across organizations. What data problems do you have?

Recording and sharing the consequences of your poor data and information makes good sense. People often say they are data rich but information poor. So it makes sense to record the consequences, but it also makes sense to record and share what your organization could do with their data if they had a higher level of confidence in the data.

The clear message from this step is to document and report the negative consequences of continuing to behave in the manner that brought on the data intervention, as well as the positive consequences that will result from becoming more disciplined around how you manage your data and information.

Choose a Location and Time

This step may not seem important until you try to schedule a time for the data intervention team to discuss how they will address the issues and opportunities. The truth is that this step may require repeated meetings, which will cause people to hesitate to become part of the team.

Data governance best practices typically suggest that senior leadership must support, sponsor, and understand the activities associated with data governance. Scheduling the location and time becomes easier when you leadership's support and you have documented the consequences mentioned in the previous step.

Senior leadership must understand how data governance will be set up, who will be involved, the amount of time it will take, and the results of governed data. This goes way past supporting and sponsoring a data governance program. The data intervention team must focus on doing whatever it takes to get leadership to understand how data governance operates or will operate. This requires a time and place to hold meetings to present the documented consequences to senior leadership.

Have a Rehearsal

This is a step defined on wikiHow for "How to Perform an Intervention." I am not certain that a rehearsal is necessary when planning a data intervention within your organization. Still, it emphasizes that it makes sense to be well-prepared before you start your data intervention.

Make certain that you select people that want or need to become part of a solution. People that are part of the problem will be addressed once the data governance program has been defined and the root causes of data problems become more apparent. The problem people may not be too difficult to find. The people passionate about improving your organization's data landscape may be more difficult to convince. Maybe not. It depends on how people feel about your present state. Be able to spell out the consequences mentioned earlier in these steps. The Boy Scout motto was "Be Prepared" years ago when I was a young lad. So, *be prepared;* this is the best advice I can give in preparing you for a data intervention. If you need to hold a rehearsal, so be it.

Hold the Data Intervention

Now we hold the data intervention. Whether or not you call the meeting a data intervention is up to you. The word "intervention" solicits mixed responses. This is especially true for those who recognize that they have a problem and are fearful of what it will take to solve it. Some people will think the term is "catchy" and attend the first meeting for curiosity's sake, while others may think it is not an appropriate use of the term.

You may want to call it an enterprise data working team as part of a formal set of data governance roles and responsibilities. Or you may want to call it a data governance planning team. It is up to you. Although the idea of formal data governance does not evoke thoughts of positive actions, it should if people are asked and tell you what they would do with the data if they had data that they trust.

Key Messages

The idea of preparing for a data intervention, documenting and sharing the consequences of poor data, and having the appropriate people involved in solving the problem may be what you need to get started. Consider holding a data intervention by following the steps outlined in this essay if one is necessary in your organization.

Perspective: To Own or Not to Own Data

To own data or not to own data, that is the question. This question often comes up when speaking with clients or groups of people during my data governance webinars and conference presentations.

Many organizations use the term "data owner" instead of "data steward" to describe people's relationship to the data. The semantics of "owner" versus "steward" drives many conversations. The question becomes, "Who truly owns the data?" The answer is often that the organization owns the data, not the individual.

The definition of a data steward that I use (and a core concept of the Non-Invasive Data Governance approach) focuses on formalizing accountability for data resources. A person is a data steward if they are held formally accountable for their relationship with the data. The relationships are 1) as a person who defines the data, 2) as a person that produces the data, and 3) as a person that uses the data.

A person is a data steward if they are held formally accountable for their relationship with the data.

The truth is that almost everybody in the organization defines, produces, and/or uses data as part of their job. The reality is that these people, for the most part, are not being held formally accountable for how they define, produce, and use data. Everybody is a data steward, yet the stewards do not even recognize themselves as such. Getting the stewards to recognize themselves as stewards is part of the job of the data governance manager or the person(s) responsible for implementing the program.

Stewards do not, in fact, "own" the data, but rather they take care of it for the organization. Just like a babysitter takes care of the kids and (hopefully) returns them safely at the end of the evening, the data steward takes care of data for the period in which they are related to the data as a definer, producer, or user of the data. When the babysitter leaves, so does their responsibility.

Over the years, I could just imagine Friday night's babysitter arguing with Saturday night's babysitter over who owns my kids. Although there may have been times when I wished this were true (not really), the truth is, the babysitters only have responsibility for the kids when they are in charge of taking care of them. Just like the data steward only has accountability when the data is under their "watchful eye."

Ok, ok...that is a silly comparison. Or is it? When a babysitter arrives to watch the children, they are basically charged with **SPECIFIC** accountabilities, not **ALL** accountabilities. They are supposed to keep the kids safe and happy, get them in their pajamas, and force them into bed. Predefined actions are the basis of their accountability. The babysitter is not responsible for seeing that homework is completed. The babysitter is not responsible for teaching kids their ABCs or educating them about right from wrong. They are accountable for actions that are plainly defined ahead of time so there are no questions about their responsibilities. Just like data stewards should be.

The people responsible for defining specific data must have formal accountabilities related to defining that data. These individuals only have the accountability for the data they define. Responsibilities for defining data include creating and maintaining data definitions for the organization, ensuring integrity and quality of the definitions, following data definition standards, and communicating concerns, issues, and problems with data definition to the individuals that can influence change.

The people responsible for creating, modifying, or deleting specific data have accountabilities related to these actions. Responsibilities of data producers include the integrity and quality of the data handled by that department. The people that produce data are responsible for the data's completeness and timeliness, management and control, and communicating concerns, issues, and opportunities to the individuals that can influence change.

The people responsible for consuming specific data have accountabilities related to data usage. For example, responsibilities for consuming data can include accountability for who can see the data and how the data can be shared. Responsibilities for data usage can include communicating new and changed business requirements to impacted individuals, and communicating concerns, issues, and opportunities around data consumption to individuals that can influence change.

Stewardship often fails because of complexities not discussed when defining how people will be held formally accountable for their actions with data. One complexity to address is planning how you will describe that everybody (or almost everybody) is a data steward. Another complexity is planning for different levels of stewards with different levels of responsibilities like the operational stewards and tactical subject matter experts stewards described in section three of this book. Planning to handle these complexities becomes the true guts of data stewardship.

Consider these items when defining data stewardship as part of your data governance program:

- Definition of roles and responsibilities.

- Procedures for collecting data about the data stewards. In other words, those people that have formal relationships to the data and keeping that information up to date.

- Selling the need for stewardship to the organization and ensuring that people recognize the importance of formal accountability.

- Procedures for stewards to resolve data-related issues and address data opportunities.

Key Messages

Companies squabble over the semantics of whether the stewards actually own the data. "Ownership" implies that the steward can do anything they want with the data. People don't own data; they take care of it. Like a babysitter.

If we aren't going to use the term "steward" instead of "owner," I'd rather see us use the word "babysitter." Consider the steward to be the Data Babysitter. The stewards responsibilities and accountabilities must be directly connected to the actions that they take with the data.

Perspective: Truth in Data—Buyer Beware

The formal governance of data results in people having confidence in the data they define, produce, and use to make decisions and direct their daily functions. Confidence in data comes from having a validated and available description of data. However, data reported to the general public is often unvalidated, and a full description of the data is not made available as the data is being reported.

The result is that data is often reported that purposefully misleads or redirects opinion. The trust in the data that is reported can be challenged. The lack of validated definition and availability of the data's definition wears away at people's trust. The old saying, "you can get the data to say whatever you want it to," holds true. Especially when the data definition is only partially accurate or doesn't match the expectations of the data consumer. There is truth in data, but the buyer better beware.

To quote a classic movie, *Network*, "I am as mad as hell, and I am not going to take this anymore!" I am wondering if you are too. The news seems discouraging, or at least that's what the news programs want you to believe. Unfortunately, there is not much good news to talk about. In addition, I *am* mad about how the press reports data associated with the news.

Sensationalism has become commonplace. The issue is how data is reported and not reported. Data can always be altered to suit the narrative of the reporter. If the reporter wants to sell you something, they will report the data so that you believe that "four out of five doctors recommend" that you use their product.

Regarding the recent virus, cases were reported as "dramatically on the rise" when the rate of infection had reached a pinnacle and had begun to fall. I am not saying that either of these statements were incorrect. However, they tell an incomplete truth.

While data is necessary to support facts, many untruths can become byproducts of how people use data. In 2012, Fast Company, a magazine focused on technology and business, published *Seven Ways to Lie with Statistics and Get Away With It*[12] where they stated the common ways to spread untruths:

- Biased sampling—this involves polling a non-representative group.

- Small sample sizes—sweeping statements become suspect when the sample size is very small.

- Poorly-chosen averages—averaging values across non-uniform populations.

- Results falling with standard error—a survey can only be as accurate as its standard error.

- Using graphs to create an impression—graphing data creatively provides room for creating false impressions.

- The "semi-attached figure"— means stating one thing as proof for something else.

- "post-hoc fallacy"—incorrectly asserting that there is a direct correlation between two findings.

One example of data being reported in such a manner dates back to a finding in The National Review Magazine in 2015 and reported in the Washington Post.[13] It demonstrated in a chart that there had been only a minor increase in the average global temperature over a 235-year period (1880-2015). Climate change is a hoax promoted by several publications that want people to believe that the minimal changes in our planet's temperature are not impacting life as we know it.

However, data from numerous other sources demonstrate that the slightest rise in temperature can cause the flooding of coastal cities, loss of the world's glaciers, extinction of marine life, etc. The list of impacts climate change has on our life

---

[12] https://www.fastcompany.com/1822354/7-ways-lie-statistics-and-get-away-it.

[13] https://www.washingtonpost.com/news/the-fix/wp/2015/12/14/why-the-national-reviews-global-temperature-graph-is-so-misleading/.

on earth is endless. The data can be downplayed as a tiny change while the impact of this action can be devastating. That is the truth in the data.

Another example is the way news stations reported the number of cases of the coronavirus versus the number of people being tested. The number of positive cases went up quickly, but the percentage of people testing positive was going downward. Most people expected that the number of cases would increase dramatically when the number of people being tested increased as well. And that was exactly what happened. So, when it is reported that the number of cases has doubled—that is bad—but what is missing is what is not reported. What is not being reported turns this data into more digestible information, perhaps less sensational and less terrifying to the average listener. A statistic that would be much more meaningful is the percentage of people tested who have tested positive. If the percentage of people who have tested positive increases, that signals that more people being tested are sick, and the percentage of people being tested is increasing. This tells us that we need to test more people to see a realistic number of positive cases we can expect. This statistic provides a better model for planning and preparing for the increased numbers.

For example: * These numbers are entirely fictional with percentages being approximate.

	Sample Virus Data	1	2	3
A	Total People	100	10,000	100,000
B	People Tested	40	350	30,000
C	Percentage of People Tested	40%	35%	30%
D	Number of People Tested Positive	10	80	6,000
E	Percentage of People Tested positive	25%	22%	20%
F	Number of People Tested Positive Deceased	2	17	1,575
G	Percentage of People Tested Positive Deceased	20%	17%	13%
H	Number of People Tested Positive People Deceased Minority Category	1	6	450
I	Percentage of Tested Positive People Deceased Minority Category	50%	35%	28%

Figure 2-1. Data Sample for Virus Cases

When we look at the numbers in the B row, we see that the number of people being tested is increasing, which is good. However, when we look at the C row, we see that the percentage of total people is decreasing, which is not as good. When we look at the D row, we see that the number of people testing positive is increasing, which is bad. However, when we look at the E row, we see that the percentage of people being tested positive is decreasing, which is good. From Row F, we see that the number of people that have died from the virus is growing rapidly, which is not good. But from G row, we see that the percentage of people testing positive and dying is decreasing, and that is more encouraging. From Row H, we see that the number of African Americans tested positive and dying from the virus is increasing, and, again, that information is terrible and frightening. However, when we look at Row I, we see that the percentage of people in that segment that are dying is decreasing.

Simply stated, by adding the percentages to the table above, you can see that the statistics provide a more telling story. The news is not great by any stretch, but this data gives the public (and potentially the news outlets) more accurate information to report.

Key Messages

There is significantly more to this story. This essay aimed to demonstrate that people can report data that defends a narrative that supports their goals and intentions. The reporting of data is not always complete, which can lead to a lack of confidence and trust in the data.

The governance of data does not always control the messaging being delivered or received by the data that is reported. Whether someone is trying to sell you something with only a small percentage of the information or a news station sensationalizes a story by providing you with an incomplete amount of data that will keep you tuned in for more information, we are all consumers of data. We are all recipients of statistic reported in a way that minimizes the true impact a change in data represents. More importantly, we are potential victims of how the data is presented to sway us.

It is imperative to be smart and to continue to demand truth in data. "Buyer beware" or "Caveat Emptor" is an expression used as a disclaimer of warranties. It arose from the fact that buyers typically have less information than sellers about the good or service they are purchasing. Truth in data comes to people who seek out "the rest of the story."

Support and Value

In my first book, I shared best practices for setting up a formal data governance program. The number one best practice focused on gaining and maintaining senior leadership's support, sponsorship, and understanding of data governance and the activities of governing their enterprise's data. Included in the understanding is the business value that will result from delivering a formal data governance program.

The chapters in this section focus on lessons learned and perspectives gained over years of helping organizations to establish and build on their leadership's levels of support and sponsorship while providing leadership with proper context and achievable expectations. Leadership needs to know where data governance fits into an overall data strategy and why they should care. In addition, leadership must understand how to improve their "data situation" (see earlier perspective essay), the connections between data and the bottom line, what their employees cannot do, and avoid common mistakes when implementing a formal data governance program. You will find essays focused on these topics in this section.

CHAPTER 3

Support and Sponsorship

The term *data governance* can be intimidating to everybody, including the people at the highest level of your organization. It is up to the program's practitioners, administrators, and champions to change that perspective. Calming leadership's fears and getting them to ask the right questions about their data is part of that change. Helping them to understand where data governance fits into the overall management of data and teaching them that data governance can be made "fun" also helps to change their perspective. Addressing support and sponsorship when a program is stumbling is important in managing change.

In this chapter, I include essays focused on influencing the perspective of people at all levels of the organization, specifically targeting the executive and strategic levels. This chapter addresses elements of a data strategy, how Chief Data Officers and others at their level of influence should stop asking why data governance is important, and instead begin asking how data governance will work and how a formal program will add value. In this chapter, you will learn how to address a failing program and how to calm management's fears of governing data. The essays in this chapter focus on improving understanding which leads to ongoing support and sponsorship.

Experience: CDOs Should Be Asking "How" and Not "Why"

The secret lies with data governance. The Chief Data Officer (or whoever the Data Czar is at your organization) needs to get past the "Why is data governance important?" or "Why do we need data governance?" questions if they are ever going to be successful czaring the data. Rather, the CDO should ask, "How are we going to govern our data?"

Individuals at many organizations spend large amounts of energy trying to convince their leadership to invest in the formal governance of data and information. Sometimes multiple people or groups are all pushing in the same direction. Some of these groups successfully convince leadership that attention must be paid to improving the organization's value from their most important asset: data.

What does it take to get senior leadership to buy-in to data governance and the need to apply resources for better data management? The answer may be in their belief that data is an asset and will not manage itself. Just because your organization is successful now doesn't mean that you cannot become even more successful by becoming more efficient and effective in using data and information.

The CDO should ask, "How Are We Going to Govern Our Data?"

There are many reasons why organizations decide to put formal data governance in place. Some auditors and examiners tell the CDO they need to demonstrate formality in how people are accountable for the data they define, produce, and use. These organizations are not given a choice to elevate the governance of data to a formal practice.

Other organizations decide to put formal data governance programs in place because they have invested (or are investing) heavily in new or upgraded data resources and systems targeted at improving the value they get from their data. Many organizations invest to improve their ability to analyze their data only to find that the data that will feed these investments is ungoverned or not of high quality.

Other organizations put policies in place to ensure that their data, information, records, and even metadata are owned and stewarded as valuable assets to be leveraged. These top-down decisions to govern the data are typically only successful when a well thought-out and practical solution is *approved* and followed as a course of action.

That's right...I said approved. This brings me back to gaining senior leadership buy-in for improved formality in how the organization governs their data.

Gaining Senior Leadership Buy-In

Gaining senior leadership buy-in requires that the person seeking approval has a well thought out plan for how the organization will maximize the value of the organization's data through data governance. An early step is to recognize that there are several different approaches that an organization can take to implement data governance. I have shared the three approaches earlier in the book, which are worth repeating from the perspective of gaining buy-in from senior leadership.

The Command-and-Control governance approach is a top-down "you will participate" approach. I call it command-and-control because this method of implementing data governance forces people to participate whether or not they understand the value that data governance will bring. It is presented as a new add-on to people's regular "day jobs."

The Traditional governance approach is what I often refer to as the "Field of Dreams" approach. The tag line from that movie was "if you build it, they will come" and that describes precisely how a program like this operates. Policy, structure, roles and responsibilities, processes, etc., are all set up, but people are not incentivized to play their role or follow the described processes.

The Non-Invasive governance approach takes into consideration that accountability for data already exists (informally), and that the formalization of accountability is based on people's relationships to the data. If a person defines data, they have accountability for its definition. If they produce data, they are held formally accountable for how they produce it (or how it is produced). And the same holds true for people that use data. Anybody in the organization that defines, produces, and/or uses data (and that can be practically everybody or anybody) needs to be held formally accountable for how they define, produce, and use data. This takes education, training, and a well-thought-out method for incrementally building this across the organization. And perhaps most importantly, this approach follows the idea that "you are already doing this" and helps people perform their function in a way that is in the organization's best interest.

"How" Approaches to Data Governance

Here is a bulleted list of the key differentiators in the "How" of implementing data governance:

The Command-and-Control Approach

- People are *assigned* roles.
- Data governance is new to the organization—all new processes.
- You *will do* what the program says.
- Measure value through return on investment directly from DG.
- Purchase software tools first and mold the approach to purchase.

The Traditional Approach

- People are *identified* into roles.
- Data governance is a single process to apply in multiple ways.
- You *should do* what the program says.
- Measure value through the improvement in the quality of the data.
- Leverage existing tools first and fill capability gaps with new tools.

The Non-Invasive Approach

- People are *recognized* into roles based on their relationship to the data.
- Data governance applies to existing or new processes.
- You are *already doing* this, and formal DG will help you to do it better.
- Measure advancement from the present state (benchmark early).
- Leverage existing tools first, develop tools as needed, and acquire them based on requirements.

Key Messages

Data governance practitioners must help their leadership to get past asking questions about why data governance is necessary and on to asking questions about how the organization is going to govern its data. Leadership is investing heavily in technologies that are focused on maximizing the value the organization gets from its data. The quality of the data, and the confidence the organization has in the data, will be determining factors in whether or not they will see the expected return on their investments. This should answer the "Why" question. Now we move onto the "How" question.

Experience: Elements of a Data Strategy

Several organizations have asked me to assist them with constructing a new data strategy or reviewing and evaluating their existing data strategy. These exercises allowed me to research the primary elements of an official and formal data strategy artifact. This essay focuses on the primary elements of a data strategy, the business case for a data strategy, the risks of not having a comprehensive data strategy, and a layout for a formal data strategy. I hope this essay will provide a good starting point for you and your organization when it comes to delivering an organizational data strategy.

Data Strategy Element Definition

A data strategy is a thorough plan and policy for moving an organization towards a more data-driven culture. Many organizations view a data strategy as a technical exercise. However, a modern and comprehensive data strategy addresses more than just the data. The strategy is a roadmap that defines people, processes, and technology. Through the data strategy, data leaders address which employees need to maximize the value they get from the data. Leaders use new data strategies to formalize data processes and correct course to ensure that high-quality and trusted data is accessible, and technology is leveraged to enable the business to gain value efficiently and effectively from their data. Organizations should consider including the following primary elements in their data strategy:

- Alignment with the business objectives of the organization. The strategy should outline how data can be used to achieve the objectives and how data can be used to support the overall business strategy.

- Definition of clear goals and objectives for data management and use. The strategy must view the organization's business requirements and strategic goals of leveraging data as a valuable corporate asset, including understanding the questions the business needs to answer with data and metadata.

- Delivery of data governance based on stewardship or what I define as formalized accountability for data. The strategy must include the application of formal data governance focused on employee behavior that allows confident enterprise-level sharing of effective data.

- Establishment of clear roles and processes for data management. The strategy must include a clear definition of the people and processes necessary to deliver on the strategy, including organizational structure, skill sets, and how they work together.

- Establishment of guidelines for data analysis and application. The strategy must provide a focus on turning data into insights and visualization, including better inventorying and cataloging of primary data assets, decision-making, and storytelling.

- Focus on the data lifecycle management or the processes and procedures for managing data from creation to deletion. The data strategy must outline the data lifecycle management framework that will be used to manage data throughout its lifecycle.

- Focus on the quality of the data, or the accuracy and reliability of data that is critical to the success of any data-driven initiative. The data strategy must outline the processes and procedures for ensuring data quality, such as data validation and data cleansing.

- Definition of a data architecture that provides the design of the data environment, including the types of data to collect, the format in which to store the data, and the tools and technologies to manage the data. The data strategy must define the data architecture to support the business objectives.

- Focus on data analytics is the process of analyzing data to derive insights that can inform business decisions. The data strategy must outline the analytics capabilities required to support the business objectives, including the tools and technologies used to perform the analysis.

- Inclusion of data security and data privacy to protect data from unauthorized access, use, disclosure, or destruction. The data strategy must include a data security framework that outlines the processes and procedures for ensuring data security, such as access controls and encryption.

- Definition of technology as an enabler of strategic success. The technology requirements, including a flexible and scalable design of systems and data resources.

- Delivery of an actionable plan to complete the strategy. The strategy must include an action plan and roadmap of the steps to move from the current to the future state.

Business Cases for Data Strategy

Not all organizations require a data strategy. The answer to whether or not a data strategy is necessary must come from the senior leadership within each organization. However, data practitioners and data leaders within an organization can influence senior leadership's decision by making a strong business case for why a strategy is needed and the risks associated with not having a strategy.

A clear understanding of your organization's vision and goals and the priorities of the organization's senior leadership sets the context for a data strategy business case. Explaining how a comprehensive data strategy can deliver business outcomes is the key to making a business case applicable and convincing.

A business case for data is a case for transformation. When making a case for change, the change must be defensible. Identify costs plaguing the organization and lost opportunities in your present situation. While your ability to quantify financial return may be a strong consideration, there is likely room for improvement through elevated data governance, data management, and data-driven capabilities.

The volume and variety of structured and unstructured data your organization manages grow exponentially. Organizations that can harness this explosive growth and make it operational create significant business differentiators over their competition.

Organizations can differentiate themselves from their competition through the business case they make for establishing their data strategy. Several examples of business use cases to build a data strategy to distinguish the organization include:

- Leveraging data to power the customer lifecycle from generating interest to motivating demand behavior, from request processing and contentment to completing downstream processes like logistics, finance, and service.

- Reducing the up-and-down effect your supply chain has on inventory by providing real-time, data-driven visibility of your entire demand and supply chain with predictive insights.

- Improving employee productivity, advancement, and retention by assisting them in achieving goals through cultivating data-related learning experiences based on their existing talent and work experience.

- Making better decisions by providing a more complete picture of their operations and customer behavior. By collecting, analyzing, and using data effectively, organizations can identify trends, patterns, and opportunities they might not have seen otherwise.

- Increasing efficiency and productivity by streamlining operations and identifying areas where processes can be automated or improved. Organizations can reduce costs and improve productivity by using data to optimize workflows and eliminate inefficiencies.

- Improving competitive advantage by collecting, analyzing, and using data can have a significant competitive advantage. A data strategy can help organizations stay ahead of their competitors by providing insights into customer needs and preferences, market trends, and emerging technologies.

- Managing risk by providing insights into potential threats and vulnerabilities. By monitoring data for anomalies and using predictive analytics to identify potential risks, organizations can take proactive measures to mitigate risk and protect their business.

- Meeting regulatory requirements by ensuring that data is collected, stored, and used in a compliant manner. By establishing data governance and data privacy frameworks, organizations can avoid costly fines and reputational damage.

Risks of Not Having a Data Strategy

The risks of not having a data strategy include poor decision-making, missed business opportunities, inefficiencies and ineffectiveness, increased risk, and potential compliance issues. It is fundamental for organizations to develop a clear data strategy that aligns with their business objectives and addresses the risks associated with managing the organization's data. Not having a data strategy can pose several risks to an organization, including that:

- Organizations will miss out on opportunities to gain insights into their operations and customer behavior. This will make it difficult to identify trends, patterns, and opportunities that could be used to improve the business.

- Organizations will make decisions based on incomplete or inaccurate data. This will lead to poor decisions that can negatively impact the business.

- Organizations will have inefficient processes for collecting, storing, and using data. This will result in wasted time and resources and may prevent the organization from realizing the full value of its data.

- Organizations will be more vulnerable to data breaches, cyber-attacks, and other security threats. This will lead to financial losses, reputational damage, and legal liabilities.

- Organizations will struggle to comply with regulatory requirements related to data privacy, security, and governance. This will result in fines, legal action, and reputational damage.

When an organization decides that a data strategy is unnecessary at the enterprise level, it is not uncommon for individual parts of an organization to contemplate more locally and deliver a strategy for the data under their management. As the breadth of a data strategy increases from being local to covering the enterprise, the overall influence of the strategy increases and can potentially incorporate a more encompassing set of people, processes, and technology.

Layout for a Data Strategy

Last but not least, my final elements of a data strategy include the layout of the sections to consider for inclusion within a data strategy. I teach this layout, or one very close to this layout, in the Carnegie Mellon University Chief Data Officer Executive Education program where I am a faculty member. You should customize this layout for a data strategy, the primary elements and business case for your data strategy, and the risks associated with not having a data strategy, to align with your organization's overall business strategy.

A comprehensive outline for a data strategy will include:

- Executive Summary – A brief outline of the data strategy, its commitment, and expected outcomes.

- Introduction – An introduction to the organization, its mission, and how data can support the achievement of that mission.

- Vision and Goals – A statement of the organization's vision for data and the goals it hopes to achieve through the data strategy.

- Current State Assessment – An assessment of the organization's current data assets, including data sources, data quality, data governance, and data management practices.

- Gap Analysis – An analysis of the gaps between the current state and the desired future state of the organization's data strategy.

- Strategy and Action Plan – A comprehensive plan for achieving the vision and goals of the data strategy.

- Implementation Plan – A detailed plan for implementing the data strategy, including timelines, milestones, roles and responsibilities, and resource requirements.

- Monitoring and Evaluation Plan – A plan for monitoring and evaluating the effectiveness of the data strategy, including performance metrics, benchmarks, and evaluation criteria.

- Conclusion – A brief summary of the data strategy, its expected benefits, and the next steps for implementation.

- Appendices – Supporting documentation, such as policies, procedures, guidelines, and technical specifications.

Experience has shown me that all relevant stakeholders, including executives, IT staff, data analysts, and business leaders, should be asked to provide input into the data strategy. The strategy must be reviewed and updated regularly to reflect changes in the organization's goals, data assets, and technological landscape.

Key Messages

Without an overall vision and foundation for the organization's data, parts of the organization will autonomously view data-related capabilities and capacity. This independence leads to duplication of data and data systems across the organization, making it difficult to determine the 'truth' from data while driving up operational efficiency and effectiveness costs. A data strategy provides the basis for enterprise planning efforts connected to data-related capabilities. A more detailed and comprehensive data strategy will improve the chances that the business and technical parts of the organization will fully understand and work in coordination and cooperation with each other.

Experience: What It Means to Make Data Governance Fun

The words "data governance" and "fun" are seldom spoken together. The term data governance conjures images of restrictions and control that result in an uphill challenge for most programs and organizations from the beginning. I define data governance as the "execution and enforcement of authority over the management of data." Sounds fun, doesn't it?

Yet data governance, and the need to raise stakeholder confidence in data, are typically serious subjects, especially if your business divisions are struggling to gain value from data. Or they are spending too much time preparing the data for proper use. Or the data potentially puts them at risk every day. These are serious challenges!

The journey from ungoverned to governed data is not without pain. Change is rarely easy or welcome. Often, leaders are under pressure to help people use data as a strategic asset but struggle with low levels of trust in that data. How can they make the change less painful? Accountability is easier when it is informal. Documentation has always been an afterthought. Is it possible to alleviate some of these pains, or dare I say, make data governance fun?

The answer is "yes"—to the "alleviate the pain" part of the question. Improving data intelligence through the automation, distribution, stewardship, and effective use of business and technical processes and metadata will certainly alleviate many of the pain points associated with governing data.

And yes, it is possible to make governance fun. This blog focuses on four key ways that organizations have made their data governance programs fun, entertaining, enjoyable, and competitive, while holding closely to their definitions of data governance.

Gamify Governance

Organizations have made data governance fun by gamifying their governance program (or turning it into a game). An extension of this is to look at data governance as a puzzle with pieces that must be completed to solve a problem.

Some organizations have voiced concern that turning data governance into a game may decrease the perception of its importance or reduce the seriousness of the task at hand. Therefore, attention must be paid to the messaging associated with gamifying data governance, ensuring that the four ways addressed here are understood in terms of the business value they add.

So, what does this look like in practice? Some organizations have imitated the youthful contest of "Capture the Flag" by gamifying the concept into "Capture the Steward" and "Capture the Business Term." These games are targeted at collecting and making available metadata that will enable people to find data and the people accountable for the data. Other organizations have turned their data governance frameworks into Bingo boards to incentivize participation, later recognizing departments that complete squares with prizes.

Engaging people in your program is critical, and fun approaches abound. Data governance programs have implemented interactive surveys to engage people to vote on appropriate decisions or watch data governance-related videos and guess the correct answers to questions—while tallying scores and rewarding people for their interaction. Viewing and interacting with content can be rewarded to encourage people to become more data literate.

Gamifying data governance requires imagination and innovation. These activities benefit greatly from working with your organization's communications, marketing, and change management specialists to gain assistance in getting the messaging right. These activities also require patience and tolerance from leadership as their attitudes and behavior toward data evolves.

Make Stewarding Something People Want to Do

People are busy with their day jobs. It is therefore important to connect what they are *already* doing with what is needed more formally instead of making data governance about a brand-new set of activities. People are already data stewards if they have an association with data and they are held formally accountable for the actions they take with data. Those actions include defining, producing, and using data.

Once people realize that they are already stewards of the data, the challenge is to get them interested in putting their best efforts into how well they define, produce, and use the data. Data governance programs can provide guidelines and detailed instructions on how to use data the way it is intended and allowed to be used (and not used). Aligning business to data definitions (and making templates and tools actionable) will help people produce more accurate insights and metadata. Data stewards require direction and definition for how they take action with data.

Data governance leaders cannot assume that people will establish quality and governance habits without guidance from the program or some other source. Data governance programs must provide frameworks, policies, guidelines, and standards that are shared with the businesspeople of the organization for these people to actively govern the data they define, produce, and use. This must then be checked and elevated on a regular basis. It can't be a one-and-done.

Programs must also communicate the value of WIIFM ("what's in it for me") from the perspective of every individual the program engages. This includes sponsors, management, owners, and stewards. Therefore, organizations must know who these people are, record those details, and make that information available. People must understand the benefits they, and the organization, will receive from the improved definition, production, and use of data. This knowledge will encourage people to get involved. Eventually, tying this into visible individual and team objectives will make it most seamlessly part of the steward's day-to-day work.

Create Friendly Competition

The third way to make data governance fun is to create friendly competition. This can be both a challenge and reward when applied to data in the workplace. Competition can lead to improvements in how your data is governed.

Organizations have advanced data documentation and stewardship levels by revealing departmental efforts and rewarding the departments that show the most improvement. Organizations have apportioned resources to projects demonstrating the highest level of preparedness, education, and data discipline. Governance activities that extend beyond departmental "norms" can be measured and included in the competition.

However, competition requires the coordination of activities to compare and report how parts of the organization govern their data. These comparisons (and how they are judged) must be meaningful in terms of business value, urgency, and often, quantifiable results. These comparisons must also reward all positive activity and not just that of the victors.

Organizations generate friendly competition in several ways. Competition focused on the definition, production, and data usage make up most of the examples. Competition can be based on the number of Critical Data Elements (CDEs) defined by divisions and departments, or the number of stewards recognized and onboarded, or the inventory, quality, and management of data resources, reports, and data projects. Friendly competition is often based on quantifiable measures attributable to people and groups. Organization-wide dashboards that show progress on a cadence are successful at creating engagement. After all, no one wants to be part of the team that's lagging behind!

Another way to craft friendly competition is to identify individuals or groups that have accomplished milestone tasks, recognizing these people for the governing actions they have taken. Organizations have gone so far as anointing people as "deputy" data stewards (complete with a silver badge), highlighting a "steward of the month" or "department of the month" as an individual or group that has a measurable impact on the governance of data across the organization.

There are several ways to report the results of friendly competition. The only limitation is an organization's imagination and willingness to explore unique ways to share. Examples of ways organizations have publicized results include through the data catalog, the "home" page for your data governance program, organizational announcements, all-hands meetings, and the use of monitors or signage that recognize the person(s) or group(s) as winners or leaders.

Provide Rewards and Recognition

The final way to make data governance fun is to recognize and reward people in a way that entices, encourages, entertains, and amuses while educating people on the value of formally governing their data.

Rewards do not need to be financial. Meaningful rewards like recognition amongst peers, additional time-off, dress-down days, departmental celebrations, and other similar incentives have been used successfully for years. Other non-financial rewards may include improved quality of data leading to improved departmental decision-making, a better understanding of and confidence in the data, and more knowledge of available data—wait, these are all rewards of well-governed data! You get my point.

Recognition must be based on positive business outcomes. These outcomes result from resolving issues and addressing opportunities to improve. Beyond recognition through reward, shared internal recognition of the value gained by the person(s) and department(s) leads to other people and departments asking, "If the data governance program assisted them that way, can data governance assist me (and my department) that way as well?" This perception enhances the favorable view of data governance within the organization.

---

*In terms of reward and recognition, there is not always a single winner.
The true winner of making data governance fun is the organization.*

Key Messages

The word "governance" implies domination and control. Data governance sounds scary, difficult, and invasive because it implies restriction, control, and constraint around data. The truth is that the data will not govern itself. The data will not protect itself, improve in quality, enhance people's confidence, and improve efficiency and effectiveness on its own.

The same can be said about metadata—that data that enables people to gain value from their data. If people need to govern, making it bearable and even fun. This "fun" direction is one that many organizations should consider taking.

This essay focused on what it means to move away from the invasive implications of governance to make data governance more fun and less imposing to the organization. Consider turning data governance into a game, building directed stewarding practices into people's jobs, creating internal friendly competition, and rewarding people for how they govern data to make data governance fun.[14]

---

[14] This piece originally appeared as an Alation blog and is reprinted here with permission from Alation.

Experience: Calm Management's Fears About Data Governance

Wouldn't it be great if you could simply put structure around how your organization governs your data without throwing a lot of money and resources at the problem? The truth is you can. You can effectively communicate to management that governance is already taking place, and that you can build a Non-Invasive Data Governance program around the present levels of governance. The following messages, if communicated effectively, should help management understand that there is a practical and pragmatic approach to data governance.

Messages to Share

If you are following, or plan to follow, the Non-Invasive Data Governance approach, you may want to consider sharing these five messages with management when attempting to calm their nerves about what it will take to implement an effective Data Governance program:

1. **We are already governing data, but we are doing it informally**. People in the organization already have responsibility for data – but that responsibility is informal. Being informal leads to inefficiency and ineffectiveness when it comes to managing our data. We should inventory who does what with data and provide an operating model of roles and responsibilities that best suits our organization. At some level, we will need someone with an enterprise view and responsibility for data that cuts across the silos in your organization and manages data as a shared resource. This is challenging because we don't naturally manage data as a shared and enterprise-wide resource.

2. **We can formalize how we govern data by putting structure around what we are doing now**. People in our organization work in operational, tactical, strategic, and support roles around data. We need to know who they are and put formal structure around who is responsible,

accountable, consulted, and informed about the business rules and regulations associated with the data they define, produce, and use.

3. **We can improve our data governance.** Our data governance efforts can help us improve how we manage risks associated with compliance, classification, security, and business rules affecting our data. People in our organization potentially put us at risk every day when they don't know the rules associated with their handling of data. Our efforts to improve data quality must be coordinated and cooperative across business units using the formal structure mentioned above. Quality assurance requires that operational and tactical staff can record, track, and resolve known data quality issues. Our organization can immediately improve how we communicate data by recording and sharing information about who does what with data.

4. **We do not have to spend a lot of money on data governance.** Data governance programs do not have to be costly endeavors. Depending on our approach, data governance may only cost the time we put into it. Data governance will require that one or more individuals spend the time defining and administering the program, but a large misconception is that data governance must be over and above the existing work efforts of an organization. We should avoid calling things *data governance processes* because this name gives people the impression that formal behavior around data is the "fault" of data governance rather than intentional actions that assure appropriate data related behaviors.

5. **We need structure.** The Non-Invasive Data Governance approach must not be viewed as a threat to people of our organization. Data governance will require structure in terms of the framework shared earlier that enables business and technology areas to accept formal and shared accountability for how data is governed. The participants in the data governance program already have day jobs. Data governance must add business value and not interfere with what our people do in their daily job functions. Non-Invasive Data Governance aims to be transparent, supportive, and collaborative.

The opposite of "Messages to Share" are "Messages Not to Share". The previous bullets spelled out specific ideas and concepts that will assist management to realize that data governance may not be as complex or scary as they think it is. The bullets below focus on specific messages that should be avoided or carefully included in conversations because they may have the opposite effect.

Messages Not to Share

These messages include ideas and concepts that you may want to avoid when attempting to calm management's fears about data governance:

1. **Avoid selling data governance as a huge challenge.** If your management already thinks data governance will be a major challenge, try to calm them by referring to the above messages for management. We can implement data governance in a non-threatening, non-interfering, non-invasive way. Data governance does not have to be implemented all at once. In fact, most organizations that successfully introduce data governance implement their programs incrementally. This includes the incremental scope of data that's governed domain-wise and organizationally and the level of governance of formal behavior applied to the data.

2. **Emphasize that data governance is a people solution and not a technical solution.** Although a technical component to your data governance program will likely exist, you can't purchase software or hardware that will be your data governance solution. What's more, simple tools can be developed internally to help organizations govern peoples' behaviors relative to data.

3. **Emphasize that people's behaviors are governed, not data.** Data governance formalizes people's behavior for data definition, production, and usage. The emphasis is on formalizing *people's behaviors*, not the behavior of data. Data behaves the way people behave. Technology may help you govern people's behaviors, but data does what you tell it to. Because people's behaviors are governed, many organizations consider data governance to be a process-driven discipline. That is partially true.

Getting people to do the right thing at the right time is a large part of a governance solution.

4. **Emphasize that data governance is an evolution, not a revolution.** As mentioned earlier, data governance will not be completed all at once. Different organizations transition themselves into a governed state in different ways. Some organizations focus early on critical data, or specific domains or subject areas of data. Other organizations concentrate on specific business areas, divisions, units, or applications, rather than implementing data governance across the organization at once. Still, other organizations focus on combining two or three specific domains within business units using specific applications. No single correct way exists for data governance to evolve in your organization. Nonetheless, I can assure you that employees will resist if you treat it as a revolution.

Key Messages

The way that you present data governance to your leadership matters. The person or people responsible for your program should consider the messages that should and should not be included in how they communicate at the executive and strategic levels of the organization. Following these tips may assist you leap ahead and avoid falling behind with your data governance efforts.

Perspective: Saving a Failing Data Governance Program

Data governance programs often take a long time to get started, gain momentum, and demonstrate measurable value to the organization. Over this period, programs often fail to sustain the enthusiasm that existed at the beginning of the program. There are many reasons for this. Management interest wanes, new projects grab people's interests, and workgroup meetings cease to be efficient and effective.

You may be surprised. Sometimes programs lose steam because the person in charge does not have the experience to apply best practice knowledge to the data governance solution. While other times, even the best plans and knowledge do not acquire the backing necessary to begin or maintain a program. In other words, it may not always have everything to do with the skills of the data governance practitioner.

Let's identify and address why data governance programs have difficulties becoming sustainable over lengthy periods. The initial approach to developing the program has an impact, but a lack of focus on essential program components discussed in my data governance framework (shared earlier in this book) is the true villain. Check out these considerations for ensuring long-term program health:

- Ways to Recognize That Your Program is Dying
- Core Program Components That Require Sustained Attention
- Steps to Follow to Prevent an Early Program Demise
- Ways to Extend Program Enthusiasm
- How to Assure Program Continuity and Longevity

Ways to Recognize That Your Program is Dying

One of the most important things you can do to keep your program healthy is to recognize when your program may not be going the way you want it to go. Some of these things may be obvious, while others are much more subtle. Become proactive to ensure that these signals never occur.

- Data governance is dropped as a line item at senior leadership meetings.
- No one brings issues or opportunities to data governance to resolve.
- There are competing data governance groups.
- No one is accountable for data governance.
- They have renamed your group something else, not data governance.
- The person in charge of data governance is being asked to spend a larger percentage of their time on something else.
- Your new boss doesn't understand data governance.
- Your data governance office/team has been broken up.
- You've solved all of the enterprise data issues. (Ha!)

Core Program Components Require Sustained Attention

No matter which approach you follow to address data governance in your organization, the core components discussed in the earlier framework essays must be designed and built with longevity of their purpose in mind for your program to remain healthy. These six core components sit at the heart of the Non-Invasive Data Governance framework essay covered earlier:

- Data – The asset that is being governed by the program.
- Roles – How people at different levels will be engaged as part of the program.
- Processes – How data governance will be applied as part of the program.
- Communications – Orientation, onboarding, and ongoing exchanges about the program.
- Metrics – How the value of the program is being measured.
- Tools – The instruments and technology that will be used to enable the program.

It is important to evaluate the amount of attention being paid to each of the core components from each perspective:

- Executive – People (or committee) at the highest level of the organization.
- Strategic – People that represent their business areas for the organization.
- Tactical – People that view the organization (and data) across business areas.
- Operational – People that focus specifically on the performance of their business area.
- Support – People that already participate in the governing functions of the organization.

It is also important to address each of the components from each perspective. For example, the program must address the data that is important to executives and also how the executives will access that data. This is a cross-reference of the data component at the executive level.

Another example is the tools that are available to the strategic level like the policy, guidelines, and directives. This is a cross-reference of the tools component at the strategic level. As part of the framework, each of the core components must be viewed from each of the perspectives to assure sustainability from your data governance program.

Steps to Follow to Prevent an Early Program Demise

The most important thing you can do to prevent your program from failing is to take proactive steps to prevent issues from occurring in the first place. Here is a list of steps you can take to prevent an early program failure:

- Maintain/build senior leadership's support, sponsorship, and understanding.
- Keep communications channels open.
- Build data governance into people's responsibilities.

- Solve meaningful problems.
- Measure and communicate your achievements.
- Add new governing functions.
- Continue to incrementally expand functions and areas.
- Don't ask for more than you need.
- Utilize other people's resources.
- Keep your meetings interesting.

Ways to Extend Program Enthusiasm

You are in good shape if you can build a level of enthusiasm around data governance early in the deployment of your program. If people are enthusiastic from the beginning, you are doing something right. But we all know that nothing lasts forever including enthusiasm, interest, and eagerness to participate in governing data.

It is often the responsibility of your data governance administrator to find ways to extend your program's enthusiasm. Here are some ways to keep in mind:

- Keep meetings interesting.
- Do interesting things. Gamify data governance if possible.
- Communicate early and often.
- Get your internal customers to tell people how you have helped them.
- Look at how you did/didn't gain enthusiasm in the first place.
- Reward people/management for good behavior.
- Extend your pleasantries to your suppliers/vendors.
- Make data a big thing; No, not big data.
- Always be looking for your next opportunity.

How to Assure Program Continuity and Longevity

It is always good to learn from other organizations that have successfully deployed and sustained their data governance programs for lengthy periods. Much information about how organizations have demonstrated value early in their program's life is available. Unfortunately, less information is available about how those programs continued to demonstrate this value. Practitioners should be requesting information about how to assure program continuity and longevity. I am sharing some tips and techniques you can use to ensure continued success:

- Communicate early and often.
- Stay relevant.
- Anticipate the next big thing (business endeavor).
- Demonstrate measurable business value.
- Educate your boss and their boss.
- Stay lean and mean.
- Align DG with the most heavily invested projects/programs.
- Keep people engaged.
- Follow an approach that best suits your culture.
- Constantly communicate the benefits of governed data.

Key Messages

This essay shared several considerations for actions you can take to energize a data governance program that is losing momentum. In this essay, I shared ways to recognize that action is necessary to keep your program active and provided a list of actions you can take to prevent your program from failing.

Sustainable data governance programs require that considerable effort is applied, and attention is paid, to extend people's enthusiasm about the program and to assure that the program provides ongoing governance of the organization's data.

CHAPTER 4

Demonstrating Business Value

It would be ideal if everybody in your organization had a complete understanding of the value of implementing a formal data governance program. There are still people that need to be convinced that the governance of data will benefit them directly. That connection can be made by assisting these same people to provide information about the challenges they face and what they can and cannot do with their data. In addition, there are common mistakes that organizations make when demonstrating business value and there are specific steps organizations can take to improve their data.

This chapter includes essays that focus on demonstrating the business value of a data governance program and addressing ways to convince and activate stakeholders that a data governance program is necessary. In addition, the essays address the people, process, and technology of data governance, ways to connect data to revenue, and considerations for connecting business value to why people should care.

Experience: Convincing Stakeholders That Data Governance is Necessary

You may already have a formal data governance program in place. Or maybe you are presently trying to convince your senior leadership or stakeholders that a formal data governance program is necessary. Maybe you are going through the process of convincing the stakeholders that data governance is worth their time investment. No matter your situation, you probably spend significant effort conveying why data governance is necessary and worth people's time and resources.

To start, if leadership is not convinced data governance is necessary, they likely will not allow you to pursue this as a discipline and data will continue to be managed and governed the way it has always been.

Stakeholders have heard about the need for formal data governance repeatedly over the years. Although stakeholders may say that they understand that improved analytical capabilities rely on confidence in the quality of the data, this does not mean that they necessarily support the need to have a formal data governance program.

But fear no more. I can provide you with three questions that, when answered thoroughly and honestly from a business and technical perspective, will provide the practitioners with the information they need to break down the barriers preventing the leadership and the stakeholders from being convinced that data governance is necessary.

The three questions are:

1. What can't you do that you need to do with data, because you don't have the data or trust the data enough to do it?

2. What would you do, or could you do, if you had the data to do it?

3. How can data governance address the answers to the first two questions?

Let's go through these questions one-by-one.

What Can't You Do?

People that use data as part of their job are typically glad to share their challenges of getting the data they need the way they need it to perform their job function. The obstacles people overcome often involve figuring out what data exists, gaining a solid understanding of that data, getting access to that data, understanding the rules associated with using that data, and combining that data with other data through a tiresome and repetitive process.

Often, the data consumers don't have access to an inventory of available data. The consumers don't have business glossaries, data dictionaries, and data catalogs that house information that will improve their understanding of the data, let alone the business. Gaining access to the metadata might be a problem even if it is available. People don't immediately know who to reach out to request access to the data. And the rules associated with the data (including classification and protection rules, business rules, ethical use rules, and more) are not documented in resources available to data consumers, thus making their use of the data a risk to the organization.

If you ask data consumers, casual data users, and data scientists what causes delays and problems completing their normal job, you can expect to get answers summarized in the previous paragraph. At that point, you will begin to understand the often-mentioned but rarely-proven 80/20 rule. This rule states that people spend eighty percent of their time wrangling (pulling together) data and twenty percent doing the meaningful work of analyzing, reporting, and answering questions. These problems assume that the data they need, or that will help them in their job, is available to them in the first place. Often, data is unavailable, or people's confidence in the data is so low that they would not trust the data resources even if they were available. This is a bad situation and something that can and should be addressed by governing data.

What Would You Do?

This is another critical question because it focuses on the other end of the spectrum. This hypothetical question, when asked appropriately, can lead data consumers and data scientists to consider applying innovation and new ways of thinking. This can lead to new ways to analyze the data and improved ways to make better decisions. Although this question is utopian and idealistic, data scientists are getting better and better at hypothesizing about the things they could do differently if only they had the data to do those things.

If you ask this question, you can expect answers like:

- I would model the data to produce predictive and improved forecasting analytics.

- I would combine or segregate data in ways that were never possible when less information about the data was known.

- I would enable improvements in our machine learning capabilities.

- I would have the ability to recognize patterns in the data that lead to more efficient and effective customer interaction, improved sales, risk assessments, and fraud detection.

This question leads to improved ways of making the organization data-centric, data-enabled, and data-savvy.

The problem with asking this question is that the answers will point out things that indicate (or make you feel) that you have failed to become data-centric, enabled, and savvy. But look at the positive side of the answer. If the data consumers are not asked what they would do if they had the data to do it, you may never learn the areas where you can improve as an organization. We should not cast blame since we have identified opportunities for improvement. And then the question becomes, What will you do about it? Which leads to the final question.

How Can Data Governance Address the Answers to the First Two Questions?

The questions of "what can't you do" and "what would you do", when taken seriously and answered honestly, will provoke responses that provide detailed insight into the challenges that stakeholders struggle with every day. Documenting the challenges of the stakeholders is important. Connecting the challenges to how formal governance can address the challenges is even more important.

When a stakeholder tells you that they do not know what data exists, or that they do not know which data they should be using, or that they are uncertain who has the ability to change the data, this is a sign that the documentation for the data may be limited or lacking. Data governance programs often direct resources and activities at building data documentation libraries, business glossaries, data dictionaries and data catalogs.

When stakeholders tell you that it is challenging to pull data together from multiple sources, or that their reporting activities take longer than necessary, or that they often must repeat the same action multiple times, this is a sign that the data is not available in a format that leads to efficient and effective use. Programs often direct resources at defining and building effective data resources to make stakeholder's jobs easier.

When stakeholders tell you that they know of specific data quality problems in data resources but do not know who to notify about the issues, the discipline of data governance can provide a formal process to collect quality issues as well as other data and information requests.

It is very important to make the connection between stakeholders challenges and the impact of formal governance and stewardship. Stakeholder's challenges presented by asking the questions above will not resolve themselves without the formal actions of a data governance program.

Key Messages

The relationship between the question "What can't you do?" and "What would you do?" and the results of having a governed data environment highlights opportunities to convince stakeholders why it is necessary to put a formal data governance program in place. The relationship and answers to the above questions demonstrate some of the best reasons to implement an effective data governance program.

In this day of heavy investment in becoming data-centric organizations, practitioners have to start deploying effective data governance techniques, preferably non-invasive, rather than spending most of their time trying to convince stakeholders and data scientists that data governance is necessary.

Perspective: The Trifecta of People, Process, and Technology

Have you ever been asked to summarize the benefits of data governance and the three main elements of data governance into two slides to use for an upcoming board meeting associated with your emerging program? You may say that this cannot be done. I say it is possible. Read on to learn what to include in the two slides.

Regarding the three main elements of data governance, my thoughts immediately turned to the People, Process, and Technology paradigm that has become part of business culture. These three elements are a staple of corporate slide decks everywhere.

Business Benefits of Data Governance

As many organizations evolve into digital enterprises, governed data (the results of a data governance program) lies at the heart of their transformation. Digital enterprises use governed data to improve decision-making. Governed data is the focus point for organizations looking to increase operational effectiveness and efficiency while decreasing rework, defects, and risk. Governed data is the asset to leverage to identify the most appropriate new products and services to build and sustain the customer base.

Organizations use governed data to recognize and build on the lifetime value of customers and products. Organizations leverage governed data to improve the overall customer experience. Governed data is critical to achieving any of these goals. Most organizations can work toward their business goals by improving data quality and people's confidence in the data. The business benefits of data governance can be tied directly to the organization's vision, mission, and goals.

Data that is ungoverned, and data that the organization does not trust, causes the organization to devote valuable time and resources to locate, access, understand, and manipulate data in order to use it effectively. Formal governance builds consistency, trust, and confidence in the data required to function as a data-centric or digitally transformed organization.

There are a lot of ways to list the benefits of data governance. In the first of the two slides, I would spell out the business benefits of data governance in six quick bullets:

- **Formalized accountability for data:** people will be recognized by the actions they take with data and held appropriately liable for consistently improved data oversight.

- **Improved operational efficiency and effectiveness:** value from the ability to decrease resource expenditure while achieving higher quality and confidence in the data.

- **Formalized data process:** data processes will be validated and reinforced, ensuring that people follow organizational best practices associated with governing data.

- **Consistent authority for data:** the process of ensuring consistent decision-making and prioritization of data opportunities will be enacted with responsibility and liability at the forefront.

- **Improved data quality, understanding, and confidence:** formal governance of data will result in superior value from data, information (data w/context), and metadata (data about data).

- **Reliable and auditable data risk management, protection, and compliance:** dependable examination and reporting of the organization's ability to follow the rules and laws associated with data.

The Data Governance Trifecta

In some circles, the term "People, Process, and Technology" ("PPT") refers to a methodology in which organizations balance these three elements to drive the activities of the organization. People perform work using technology to modernize and improve processes.

The PPT methodology has been around for more than fifty years. Organizations use PPT to improve the operational efficiency of their employees. Organizations consider PPT to be the basic three elements necessary to enable their successful transformation. PPT is a model for organizational improvement in almost every industry.

The first element, **people**, focuses on getting employees, contractors, advisors, consultants, suppliers, providers, and customers to engage with the data in the right way. People define, produce, and use data as part of their jobs and improvements in how they take action with the data becomes a big part of formal data governance success.

The second element, **process**, is defined by the American Society for Quality (ASQ) as a set of interrelated activities characterized by specific inputs and value-added tasks that make up a procedure to deliver a specific set of outputs.[15] When governing processes, it is essential to get the right people involved at the right time in the right way in the right process.

The third element, **technology**, focuses on the tools and techniques of data governance. This element focuses on improving the use of organizational data resources and information systems. Technology supports processes and enables the people of the organizations to operate with data efficiently and effectively. Technology is becoming the driving element that empowers organizations to seek out and achieve competitive advantage.

In the second of two slides, I suggest that you spell out the three main elements of data governance as:

- **People:** Data governance is the most effective tactic to formalize accountability for how **people** define, produce, and use data to perform their job functions.

---

[15] American Society for Quality (ASQ), http://asq.org/glossary/p.html—2014.

- **Process:** Data governance applies formality to **process** to assure consistent execution and enforcement of authority over data definition, production, and use.

- **Technology:** Using data governance **technology** (primarily business glossaries, data dictionaries, and data catalogs) will enable the organization to maximize the value of the organization's people and processes that define, produce, and use data.

Key Messages

This essay summarizes the benefits and elements of your data governance program into just two slides using the people, process, and technology paradigm. You may, or may not, ever get this request. Perhaps it would make sense for you to pretend that you have been selected to present to an executive team about your data governance program's benefits and core elements. You are given five minutes and expected to present two slides at the meeting. Now you will be prepared.

Perspective: What You Cannot Do Because Your Data is Ungoverned

I know the secret to getting business people to tell us why they need data governance. It is really quite simple. The secret is to ask them the single question, "What can't you do, that you need to do, because the data is not there to support your doing it?" An honest response to this question will provide the data governance practitioner with business cases they must address through their data governance program.

Let me break the question down for you.

What Can't You Do...

This is the loaded part of the question. Whenever you ask a person to honestly answer what they cannot do, you can expect that there will be the potential for a barrage of information. Ask the question professionally so that the answer will not lead to a complaint session. Tell the person answering the question that the goal is to improve what they can do by providing them with the data and information they need when needed.

That You Need to Do...

The second part of the question focuses on what is most important to the business. We ask what functions they require data to perform and receive answers regarding the data they require to perform their daily job function. We also learn about things they cannot do based on these requirements.

The things they cannot do may include that they 1) cannot answer certain questions, 2) cannot access data that will help them to complete their job function, or 3) cannot complete activities efficiently and effectively. Their answers will be excellent artillery to share with senior leadership.

Because the Data is Not There...

The third part of the question brings data further into the discussion. What does it mean to state that the "data is not there?" This part of the question brings the dimensions of data quality into the discussion. The data may be unavailable, untimely, low quality, inaccessible, or there may not be the metadata that is required for people to have confidence in the data. The "data is not there" means that the data does not meet their business requirements.

To Support Your Doing It

The final part of the question pulls it all together. Businesses run like efficient and effective machines, and business users can be innovative and creative when they have the resources they require to complete their job to the best of their ability. Getting business people to tell you what they need, especially the data and information they require, has been sorely understated for the many years that organizations have been developing or purchasing information systems to match their requirements.

Getting Business People to Open Up

Getting business people to open up about things they cannot do is important. Getting people to share what they would like to be able to do is also critical to the success of a data governance program. This battle between what the business needs and what the information technology people provide has been at the core of the business-IT relationship since computer systems and the use of data began.

Therefore, data governance administration must demonstrate to the business people that they are truly interested in learning about their pain points and helping them. The simple question I shared is a good first step toward understanding what the business needs. The question I shared should replace less thought-provoking questions like "What data do you need?," "How do you want your data?," or "What do you do?"

Getting business people to open up about what data and information they need to perform their job function has another benefit. The answer to the question becomes the ammunition most data governance practitioners require when approaching their senior leadership about the needs and benefits of putting a formal data governance program in place for the organization.

Connect the Answers to Data Governance

The answers to my question become why data governance is necessary for the business, but that may not be straightforward until you explain why. Making the connection between what the business cannot do because the data does not support doing it—and what data governance will do to make it such that the data and information does support what the business needs, is not easy to do.

If business people say they cannot answer certain questions, find ways to connect how formal data governance will assure that the business people have access to the data they require to answer those questions. Formal data governance can assure that the data business people access is well defined, follows standards, and meets their requirements to answer their most important questions.

If business people say that they cannot access the data that will help them to complete their job functions, find ways to connect how formal data governance can assure that the *right* data gets into the *right* hands at the *right* time. If business people say that they cannot complete activities efficiently and effectively, find ways to connect how formal data governance can assure that people will have the data and information they require, when they require it.

Key Messages

Perhaps the question that I shared at the beginning of this essay is not the perfect question for you to ask your business people. Variations on the question may be more suitable for your situation or address different angles of the same question.

Variations on the question include:

- *What can't you do that you need to do with data, because you don't have the data or trust the data enough to do it?*

- *What would you do, or could you do, if you had the data to do it?*

- *How can data governance address the answers to the first two questions?*

Experience: Connecting Data to Revenue

My strongest essays come from opportunities to work with great organizations. A long-time client recently told me that, for their data and metadata management efforts to be viewed as successful by senior leadership, improvements in these disciplines need to be directly associated with revenue increases.

This was a new demand that needed to be satisfied quickly. My client was told by their leadership that they must make the connection or risk losing funding for data and metadata management initiatives. Thus, a new and unexpected opportunity arose.

Immediately embracing the challenge, I defined, and recommended a series of steps to associate data activities with revenue increases. Here are the main steps:

- Start by recognizing where revenue comes from.
- Identify business factors that improve (or weaken) revenue gains.
- Determine the impact data and information have on these business factors.
- Articulate the connection between data and revenue.
- Direct data actions toward managing data and increasing revenue.
- Measure the changes in revenue resulting from data actions.

Recognize Where Revenue Comes From

This step appears to be easy. We all know that revenue comes from sales. The simple equation of "revenue equals price times units sold" focuses on income from sales of goods or services. For most organizations, this definition holds true but only shows a piece of the picture. Revenue can also come from secondary sources and take on different meanings depending on the context. Revenue can be projected as the expected lifetime value from a customer. Revenue can be generated through partnerships and relationships. For non-profits, revenues are determined through gross receipts. Revenue directly impacts an organization's income statement. Looking at your income statement can quickly answer revenue sources.

Identify Factors Impacting Revenue

This step is not as easy. Factors that impact revenue are often specific to the revenue source. Directing the right questions to the right people or using data to analyze cause and effect is focused on determining what influences revenue fluctuations. Factors are often data-related or found by analyzing the data itself.

Choosing the right market for revenue growth is important. Choosing the market is influenced by your data on that market, the timeliness and quality of that data, and the confidence people have in using the data to make important decisions.

Removing friction from the sales process is a factor that impacts revenue. Aligning your sales and marketing functions also impacts revenue. These factors are data-focused, as friction through poor information or misaligned sales and marketing often leads to sales decreases. Efficient sales processes and aligned business functions are often data-related and directly impact revenue.

Determine the Impact Data Has on Revenue

If your organization has not yet linked data and revenue, determining the impact requires the ability to project into the future. You can do your best to associate past data and information capability enhancements with revenue changes, but the data is often unavailable to make that connection. If you look to the future, you can benchmark your present state and report your results. For example, what will be the results of salespeople becoming better equipped with customer data and information? Will it lead to stronger customer relationships, expanding portfolios, and new revenues? Is there a way to demonstrate the effect that more information has on sales results?

What will impact direct customer revenue when your customers receive self-service access to product and service data and efficient purchasing capabilities? Data and information are precious resources that impact every line of your income statement. Identifying business factors and the data influencing them is an important step in relating data and revenue.

Articulate the Connection Between Data and Revenue

Since sales is similar to revenue, looking for a direct connection between data and sales is important. There are several ways to connect increased customer value and sales to the information you have about your customers. In one example, Amazon not only does a good job tracking what you buy and when you buy it, but they track and report to you (suggest) what other customers have purchased related to your purchases. The data has clearly demonstrated to Amazon that these connection points often lead to additional sales.

A supermarket promotes a customer loyalty program to decrease prices for regular customers, while the true value comes from the supermarket's data. The stores know what you buy, how often you buy it, when you buy it, and they also keep track of items bought together. It is common practice for supermarkets to leverage that information and to lower the cost of one item while increasing the price of related merchandise – to increase the profit margin.

In these cases, the organizations can articulate that improvement in revenue is due to improvements in data and analytics. This connection is not always obvious, and you will need evidence (in terms of cause and effect) to prove the relationship.

Direct Data Actions at Revenue

Once you have identified and documented business factors that influence revenue and recognized the impact the data and information have on these business factors, it is important to direct the actions you take to improve the management of that data.

These data actions may include implementing formal data governance and stewardship practices to assure accountability for the data's definition, production, and use. These data actions may include managing metadata associated with building confidence in data that impacts revenue-generating factors. These data actions may include developing and delivering strategic analytical platforms that permit data scientists to predict trends and study the cause and effect of revenue changes.

The most important consideration for directing data actions at revenue is to ensure that you can connect the cause (the data actions you take) to the effect (changes to revenue). This relationship is not always easy to quantify, yet it is important.

Measure Changes in Revenue

The last step of this process is to measure the impact the data actions mentioned above have on reported revenue. To accurately measure the impact of the data actions requires that you take a benchmark measure associated with each stream of revenue and observe changes to the revenue against the timing of the specific actions you take.

Key Messages

The cause and effect of data actions and changes to revenue play a large role in relating data governance and data management to financial improvements in the business. Organizations tend to focus on efficiency gains, cost reductions, and risk mitigations to relate their data actions to the organization's bottom line.

Experience: Look Out for These Six Data Mistakes

There are six repeated mistakes that organizations make when initiating their data governance or data management programs. The mistakes are not provided in any particular order. Still, they can all stand on their own as reasons why the data disciplines get overlooked or fail to meet the organization's expectations.

1. Senior leadership does not understand the resources and activities required to govern data effectively and, therefore, cannot support and sponsor data management as a valued asset. The first data governance best practice selected by many organizations is that senior leadership supports, sponsors, and understands the activities required to govern the data and the actions being taken by the people leading the program. Without this level of support, sponsorship, and understanding, there is typically a consensus that the program will be at risk of abandonment or failure.

   Data governance goals are not aligned to the organization's values and mission. Some organizations include words from their mission within their definition of data governance. For example, a recent client ends their definition with the words "to achieve operational excellence" while another directs their definition to "minimizing and eliminating data risk." One other organization included "successful governance of data and information" in their C-Level's 2022 goal, almost forcing the hand of senior leadership to understand the activities of their data governance initiative.

2. People in the business areas do not understand why they are being asked to do things differently or why extra controls associated with governing data are in place. Someone recently asked me how to get the people in his business unit to follow the data governance program activities set forth by his organization's data governance team. The term "day jobs" highlighted the conversation as the people that remain at his organization after a series of layoffs are very busy doing the jobs of several people.

People do not have time for extra work. Therefore, data governance gets a bad reputation, as being invasive. The difference between the Non-Invasive Data Governance approach and other approaches is that the non-invasive approach focuses on formalizing accountability where, in fact, the accountability has been informal, inefficient, and ineffective over the years. This approach focuses on communicating effectively with business units to help them understand the value that data governance brings to their existing job without requiring changes in priorities or asking them to do more work in the normal workday.

3. Organizations look for direct Return on Investment (ROI) from data governance rather than where their major investments lie, which is in information technology that depends on quality data. It is not impossible to demonstrate a financial return on investment directly from implementing a data governance program. It's just not easy. Organizations focus on how much they will gain versus how much they will spend when determining where to spend. That appears extra true when organizations decide where to focus resources on data disciplines.

    ROI for these disciplines is difficult to articulate. Organizations appear ready and willing to spend their resources on the latest and greatest technologies, including building out their analytical capabilities, business and artificial intelligence capabilities, big data, smart data, and integrated applications. One common requirement to provide ROI from these investments is high quality data. Organizations should look for ROI from these initiatives due to the data's availability, quality, protection, and shareability. Look at what you are getting from these initiatives, then turn up the data quality and look at the ROI again. Or recognize, in the first place, that you will never get any ROI from these initiatives unless the data is trustable, understandable, and available.

4. Roles and responsibilities associated with governing data are not defined to imitate the organization's culture and are not agreed upon by those participating in the roles. Roles and responsibilities are the backbone of a successful data governance program and must be communicated effectively and approved by management and the people filling the

roles. The roles become vital to governance accountability, processes, and communications. Organizations should be very careful in defining roles, taking extra care to make certain the roles imitate real-life within the organization.

Organizations attempt to follow data governance models that have been successful for someone else or another organization. I always suggest that rather than trying to fit your organization into the model I share, you must attempt to overlay the model over existing roles within your organization. Something that works for one organization will not necessarily work for another organization and data governance roles are often very specific to the culture of each organization.

5. Resources have not been defined to administer the governing of data, including the senior level sponsor and the person or people required to direct the effort. This aligns perfectly with another best practice that the majority of my clients define when assessing their organization's data governance maturity. As I stated earlier, one of the criteria I use for defining best practices is that the program will be at risk if the best practice is not achieved. If there is nobody to administer the program and resources are not permitted to apply their time to improving the way data and information is governed, your program will be at risk.

    Data governance does not always require a large team of people to run the program. But if nobody has that responsibility, the program will fail. Many organizations start by defining a manager, leader, or administrator for their program. That person has the early responsibilities of defining the program, goals, scope, roles, processes, communications, etc. Later, they are responsible for administering and managing the program's activities, such as working teams, councils, steering committees, and the stewards themselves. Depending on the speed at which the program implementation is expected to roll out, additional resources may be necessary to effectively cover all bases. The program will not manage itself.

6. The organization has not formally approved and communicated the goals, scope, success measurements, and expectations of governing data,

including what will change, how it will change, and the impact it will have on people. For an organization to be successful with data governance, it is important to make certain that the people in the organization, from the senior leadership level to the operational stewards level, understand the goals, scope, and expectations of the initiative. This requires that somebody in the organization be responsible for defining, vetting, and gaining approval of the data governance program's goal, scope, and expectations.

Another piece of this mistake is that people from the top to the bottom of the organization must be told what will change, why it needs to change, how it will change, and the impact the change will have on them. Many organizations define goals, scope, and expectations, but few organizations become good or great at sharing how data governance will impact people within the organization. This needs to change if we expect people across the organization to pay attention to the fact the data and information require governance. Sharing how things will change is important to staying non-invasive in your approach.

Key Messages

This essay outlines six key data mistakes that organizations make when they are getting started standing up their formal data governance program. The mistakes can happen together, or they can stand on their own as reasons why the data governance discipline gets overlooked or fails to meet the organization's expectations.

Perspective: Ways to Improve Your Data

Imagine what it would be like if your data was perfect. By perfect, I mean fit for use and high quality. By perfect, I mean that the people in your organization have confidence in the data to use it for effective decision-making and to focus on building efficiency and effectiveness through data in your operations.

You may not live in a perfect data world. And your dreams of the perfect data world might seem unachievable. If you know the concept of "continual improvement," you probably recognize that there is no perfect data world. No matter your state of perfection or brokenness, there are always ways to improve your present condition. Here are ways that you can improve your data:

- **Sell data.** By selling data, I do not mean to say that you should dress up your data and put it on the market. There are ways to make money from your data, but that is not what I mean here. By selling your data, I mean selling the need for good data (or improved data) to your organization's leadership and stakeholders. Work on convincing your leadership that these actions are necessary. An earlier essay suggested that you start by asking business people in your organization two questions and report their answers to your leaders. The two questions are 1) What can't you do because you don't have access to the data or have confidence in the data to do it? And the flip side of that question is, 2) What would you be able to do if you had access to, or confidence in, the data to do it? You can share the answers to these questions with your leadership to sell the need for improved data.

- **Plan for the data.** Take your organization's data plans or strategy off the shelf and build renewed interest in the actions, resources, and outcomes needed to improve your data situation. Your data strategy is the plan you need for using software tools, strengthening processes, formalizing accountability, and defining rules for managing, analyzing, and building value into business data. Your data strategy will help you to make informed decisions and keep your data safe and compliant. Planning for data is an important action you can take immediately.

- **Govern the data**. Governance, like government, requires a set of rules that are in place to preside over and exercise control over any situation. One such situation to consider governing is your present data situation. Ungoverned data leads to a lack of confidence in data. If people do not trust the data, the chances are that your data situation needs to be improved. Several approaches and models are available to assist organizations in governing their data. In prior essays, I wrote about the command-and-control, traditional, and non-invasive approaches to data governance. There are federated, centralized, and distributed models to consider when appropriately structuring governance to improve your data. Get started governing your data.

- **Steward the data**. Data stewardship is the formalization of accountability for data. The one phrase I repeatedly hear from my clients is that there is a "lack of accountability for the definition, production, and usage of data." Everybody that has a relationship to the data as definers, producers, or users of data, are stewards of the data if they are held formally accountable for the actions they take with data. Governance programs must educate people about stewardship and enforce formal accountability to improve data.

- **Provide metadata for the data**. Data by itself has no meaning or context. If you are provided with a piece of data, you likely will not know what that data represents without any description or information about that data. Is a number a quantity, an amount, an address, a calculated field, or something completely different? The data has no meaning until context is provided. That context, in the field of data management, is metadata. Now put yourself in the position of a corporate executive viewing their daily production dashboard, or a manager who needs to decide on data they receive in a report. These people must trust and have confidence in the data they use. That confidence comes from their knowledge about the data, or in other words, the metadata that helps the organization improve its data.

- **Communicate about the data**. Organizations that strive to become data-centric or data-driven are introducing policies that spell out that data is an asset and how it will be governed. Organizations are concentrating on changing their cultures when it comes to data and there is a push for organizations to become more data literate. Data literacy is a label given to the ability to read, understand, create, and communicate with data. Communication is a core component of successful data governance. Communications about data ranges from orienting people to the concepts and practices of managing data as an asset, to the onboarding of people in data roles such as stewards, to ongoing communications about metrics and activities focused on improving the organization's data situation. To improve the data, organizations must improve their literacy and understanding of the significance of their data management and governance efforts.

- **Protect the data**. Organizations must protect their data. Data classification and handling have become a priority while information security plays a large role in how organizations improve their data. From Personally Identifiable Information (PII) to Personal Health Information (PHI), to the protection of Intellectual Property (IP), organizations have embraced their need to secure sensitive information and data. Improvements in data often begin by securing and protecting data. The relationship between the Chief Data Officer (CDO) and the Chief Information Security Officer (CISO) has strengthened in organizations that have a strategy for delivering improved data. Organizations can learn from their efforts to protect the data when transitioning into a formally governed data landscape. Protecting data is important, but it is just one of the actions organizations can take to improve their data situation.

Key Messages

This essay spelled out several ways to improve your data. While the ways I described here may be simple concepts, the actions I share are not easy to accomplish. A journey starts with the very first step, so consider selecting a few items on the list and start taking the steps necessary to improve your data.

Organizations and Roles

One of the core messages of Non-Invasive Data Governance is that data will not govern itself. Data will not manage itself either. Organizations are finding it important to differentiate between the governance and management of data while determining the appropriate model and direction to follow for their programs. Effective data governance programs focus on an organizational design that includes the roles and responsibilities of everybody that defines, produces, and uses data as part of their everyday jobs. The ability to recognize, guide and reward stewards, and leverage the partners of data governance are important considerations for building a successful program.

This section addresses elements of stewardship critical to the organizational self-discipline that is required to effectively follow the non-invasive approach. The chapters focus on considerations for organizational design and how to build a management and stewardship-centric set of roles and responsibilities that will be most effective for your organization.

CHAPTER 5

Organizational Design

There are several models organizations can follow when designing how data governance and data management will be applied across the enterprise. There are often data management programs that must coexist with data governance programs. Organizations can follow centralized, federated, and distributed models. Organizational design and placement are very important considerations for setting up a formal data governance program.

In this chapter, I include essays that address organizational design and its influence on program success, the similarities and differences between data governance and data management, models for organizational design, who should be responsible for your data governance program, and why you may want to consider following a federated model. In this chapter, I share that there are many governing activities already taking place in your organization, but there is only one data governance.

Experience: Organizational Design and Influence on Program Success

The design of your data governance organization will influence the success and sustainability of your data governance program. Data governance is the execution and enforcement of authority over the management of data and data-related assets. The goal of the organizational design and the program itself is to ensure that data is accurate, complete, and consistent across business units and the primary information systems.

Effective data governance requires a clear understanding of roles and responsibilities, communication, and collaboration across different teams within the organizational design. This essay focuses on several important considerations for data governance program organizational design including:

- The Designing Influence
- Design Considerations
- Influence of Organization Size
- Influence of Non-Invasive Design

From my experience, effective organizational design for data governance depends on your organization's specific needs and the goals you have for your program. I hope these considerations are helpful as you design your data governance organization.

The Designing Influence

The design of an organization's structure can accelerate or obstruct the success of your data governance program. A well thought-out and planned organization is one that promotes cross-business communication and collaboration. An organizational structure designed without much planning can make the sharing of data difficult across business units and information systems, often promoting data silos.

Organizational design can impact data governance program success in several ways:

- Organizational design helps to spell out the appropriate roles and responsibilities for all levels of people involved in the data governance program. When roles are clearly defined, team members will understand their specific responsibilities and how they contribute to the success of the program.

- Organizational design facilitates communication between across the different levels of roles and responsibilities mentioned in the previous bullet. Communication is essential to ensure that team members have the information they need to make informed decisions and take appropriate actions with data they trust.

- Collaboration is essential for effective data governance. Organizational design can facilitate collaboration by promoting cross-functional teams and establishing clear communication channels. A well-designed organizational structure that promotes collaboration can help to ensure that team members work together to achieve shared goals.

- Organizational design establishes formal lines of accountability for data governance. When roles and responsibilities are clearly defined, team members can be held accountable for their actions and decisions. This can help to ensure that data is managed effectively.

Design Considerations

We can use several patterns or models of organizational designs to support effective data governance. The most appropriate design will depend on your organization's size, structure, culture, and goals. Some organizational designs to consider for data governance include:

- In a centralized organization, decision-making and control are typically concentrated in a single part of the organization. A centralized design can be effective for data governance if there is a requirement for strict oversight of data. Conversely, it can also lead to a lack of flexibility and slow decision-making.

- In a decentralized organization, decision-making and control are distributed throughout the organization. A decentralized design can be effective for data governance if there is a requirement for flexibility and quick decision-making. This model or pattern of organizational design can lead to a lack of consistency and standardization in data management.

- In a federated organization, data governance follows mostly a decentralized approach where business units maintain the responsibility for their own data governance, while still adhering to overarching enterprise-wide policies and standards. In other words, a federated model for data governance enables different business units or departments to govern their own data, but within a common framework and guidelines.

The Influence of Organizational Size

The size of your organization will significantly influence the design of a data governance program. As organizations grow larger, the complexity of their data landscape typically increases, requiring more robust mechanisms to govern data effectively. Larger organizations also typically, but not always, have resources available to devote to data governance, enabling them to implement foundational governance structures and processes.

The size of your organization will influence your data governance program due to these considerations:

- The size of your organization will influence the scope of your data governance program. Larger organizations typically have more data sources, more data types, and more data stakeholders to manage, which may require more comprehensive governance design.

- Larger organizations often have a more complex data landscape, with multiple layers of decision-making authority. This may involve establishing a centralized data governance team or committee to oversee all aspects of data governance.

- Larger organizations often require broad policies and standards that certify that data is governed effectively and consistently across the organization. These policies and standards may cover areas such as information security, data quality, data documentation, data sharing and access, and data privacy and ethical use.

- As your organization grows, sophisticated technologies are required to govern its data effectively. Addressing a larger organization often involves implementing data governance catalog platforms or other technologies to automate aspects and ensure compliance with governance policies and standards.

- As your organization or program grows, you may have more resources available to devote to your data governance program. These resources may include additional personnel, a budget for consulting services, and monies allocated for the use or data technologies.

An organization's size can significantly impact the design of a data governance program, requiring more comprehensive governance mechanisms, policies, and standards as the organization grows larger. It is important to consider the unique needs and challenges of the organization when designing a data governance program, taking into account factors such as organizational structure, resource availability, and data landscape complexity.

The Influence of Non-Invasive Design

An organizational design set up to be non-invasive aims to establish governance procedures that do not significantly burden the existing organizational structure or require substantial changes to the current business processes. A non-invasive approach aims to integrate data governance into the organization's existing workflows and decision-making processes as seamlessly as possible.

Some features of a non-invasive organizational design for data governance include:

- The application of governance into existing processes. Rather than creating new governance processes, a non-invasive approach embeds formal governance into existing business processes, such as project management or data access requests. For example, we might integrate data quality checks into the project management process rather than have a separate step to perform after the project is complete.

- A focusing on self-service. The non-invasive approach aims to empower end-users to steward data as well as possible, rather than relying on a centralized governance team to oversee all aspects of governing data.

- The ability to leverage existing roles and responsibilities. The non-invasive approach leverages existing roles and responsibilities within the organization, rather than creating new roles specifically associated with data governance. For example, a data steward or subject matter expert might be responsible for defining a specific set of quality standards for the data they govern.

- An emphasis on communication, education, and training. The non-invasive approach emphasizes communication, literacy training, and education to ensure your stakeholders understand the importance of data governance and how it fits into their existing workflows.

A non-invasive organizational design for data governance integrates governance into the existing organizational structure as seamlessly as possible, to minimize disruption and support widespread adoption. This approach requires strong communication, education, and buy-in from senior leadership, to ensure that data governance is viewed as an essential part of the organization's overall mission and goals.

Key Messages

The design of your data governance organization influences the business value that is derived from your data governance program. A well thought-out and planned organizational structure for your data governance program promotes cross-organization collaboration, communication, and accountability. A weakly designed organizational structure can promote the establishment of data silos and hinder the success of the program. You should consider your organizational design's impact on positioning your program for success.

The most effective organizational design for your data governance will depend on your organization's specific goals and requirements. Therefore, start your data governance program by assessing your organization's existing structure, culture, and processes, and identify areas where improvements can be made to support effective data governance.

Experience: Federating Data Governance

Organizations struggle with determining the appropriate level of authority to give to the people running their data governance program. Many data governance teams do not have the authority to tell business and technical areas that they must participate in governed data practices. In that case, the organization may consider adopting a federated model to implement data governance.

Notice that I called "federated" a model rather than an approach. A model refers to how the data governance program will be operationalized rather than the philosophy behind how the program is designed. My favorite dictionary definition (freedictionary.com) of the term *federated* is "to cause to join into a league or similar association." The term federated focuses on bringing together. For example, a league of sports teams is a federation because they are autonomous bodies governed and guided by a central office. DAMA International is a federation because it includes an international office providing guidelines and governance to local chapters.

In many situations, the central Data Governance Office (DGO) does not have the authority to tell the business or technical participants that they must follow procedure. If your DGO has a higher level of authority, the chances are that the model you are following is not federated. Federated data governance begins with a central DGO, a Data Governance Team (DGT), or even a single person as a data governance manager. This person or group is responsible to somebody for data governance in the organization. The size and complexity of the organization often influence the size, and often the name, of this central facilitation or governance body.

Typically, the central body provides consistent and thorough governance across the entire organization. This is where the difficulties with this model begin. The first task at hand is to address the following questions:

- How do we convince leadership that the federated model makes sense and that a central body is necessary?

- What value will the central body add to the organization, and how do we convince the business and technical areas (and their teams) of the same?

- What support will the central body provide to the "teams" as the "teams" take on the primary responsibility for their own governance?

Be prepared ahead of time to answer these questions when you suggest that the federated model is the best model for your organization. Clients have communicated the concept of "grass roots" data governance as being non-invasive but experience reliance on the ability of the organization to self-govern – or to follow standards and guidelines.

A successfully federated data governance program requires the central DGO understand the organization's needs and consider them when selecting the services that the DGO will provide. You can learn the needs by conversing with people involved in projects, programs, and processes.

In a federated model, the DGO takes on the responsibility of learning what is important to the organization and providing services focused on improving how data is defined, produced, and used as an enterprise asset. Federated data governance becomes a set of shared services the DGO provides for business and technical areas across the enterprise. It is important to define the types of assistance the central body will provide to the organization. There are several ways assistance can be provided. Each method of assistance requires significant planning and development before providing assistance. The ways to assist can fall into several categories. The main categories that I have experienced have included:

- **Data governance thought leadership and education.** Includes the research, development, and communications of the appropriate approach to govern data for your organization. The approach to data governance can include 1) implementing command-and-control over the data, 2) implementing an optional program that you hope will be followed, or 3) implementing a non-invasive approach where accountability is formalized based on people's relationship to the data (as definers, producers, and users).

- **Enterprise operating model and roles and responsibilities.** Includes developing a sensible and understandable set of roles and responsibilities that govern the definition, production, and usage of data replicated across the organization at all levels. We often call it an enterprise operating model when using the federated method.

- **Program guidance and facilitation.** Includes utilizing the enterprise operating model of roles and responsibilities based on formalizing the accountabilities for the data relationships mentioned above. We must help the definers follow the rules associated with defining data. We must help producers to understand the impact of the data they produce. Users must understand and follow the rules associated with governing and handling the data. These expectations require that someone guide and facilitate the organization toward formal data governance.

- **Best practices and maturity assessments.** Includes providing the capability to conduct cross-enterprise (or individual part) comparisons to industry or customized best practices focusing on lowering the risks associated with starting a data governance program and governing the most critical data in the area. Often these assessments result in maturity models and a detailed road map for implementing data governance in part of or across the entire organization.

- **Internally developed tools and templates.** Includes providing proven tools and templates, often in the form of internally developed instruments through Visio, Excel, and SharePoint, that help the federated teams self-govern their data while staying consistent in the context of the enterprise. Tools and templates that provide this assistance include the common data matrix, governance activity matrix, communication plan template, questionnaires, and ways to measure the value of your data governance program.

- **Enabling technologies.** Includes leveraging and enabling existing and new technologies that will assist you on the road to formally governing your data. You can use data modeling tools to enforce business definition rules, data dictionary and glossary tools to improve enterprise understanding of data, data quality tools to profile and manage the quality of data, and metadata management tools to make the metadata most useful to your organization. A centralized data governance office can aid in the consistent and quality implementation of all of the tools that currently, or will exist, in your environment.

- **Standard processes and conventions.** Includes facilitating, developing, and enforcing standard data processes within or across business functions. Standard processes include data quality issue resolution, request for access to data, and the managed integration of data from different parts of the organization. Conventions include naming conventions, definition conventions, standard use of business objects, and the rules to protect sensitive data. It is the responsibility of the DGO to document, record, and share standards, standard processes, and conventions.

- **Organizational policy and guidelines.** Includes policies and guidelines to support the enforcement of authority over the data. Governance policies and guidelines often focus on regulatory compliance, protecting sensitive data, and sharing data to improve effective use. The DGO or similar central body can provide templates for new policy, process for gaining approval of policy, assurance of access to policy, and assurance that the policies are communicated effectively across the enterprise.

- **Communication planning and delivery.** Includes developing a communications plan that addresses the business and technical interests of the enterprise. Typical communication plans ensure an appropriate orientation to data governance, onboarding of people actively involved in processes associated with governing data, and ongoing communications focused on delivering successful governance to all levels of the enterprise. The central body or DGO typically takes on the responsibility of providing consistent and quality communications about data governance across the enterprise.

- **Business glossary and metadata management.** Includes business glossaries, data dictionaries, or metadata repositories, depending on their needs and requirements for managing the metadata associated with their most critical data. This helps the organization improve its understanding, linkage, and lineage of the data from a cross-enterprise perspective. The DGO is often at the heart of developing and delivering the strategy, approach, and implementation of tools associated with governing data as an enterprise asset.

Program Guidance and Facilitation

This type of assistance includes formalizing the accountabilities for the relations people have with data. We must help the definers follow the rules associated with defining data. We must help producers to understand the impact of the data they produce. Users must understand and follow the rules associated with governing and handling the data. These types of expectations require that someone guide and facilitate the organization toward formal data governance.

Best Practices and Maturity Assessments

This type of assistance includes providing the capability to conduct analysis of where the organization compares to industry best practice focused on standing up and sustaining a formal data governance program. These assessments often result in maturity models and detailed road maps for implementing data governance for part of the organization or the organization as a whole.

Internally Developed Tools and Templates

This type of assistance includes providing proven tools and templates, often in the form of internally developed instruments through Visio, Excel, and SharePoint, that help the federated teams self-govern their data while staying consistent in the context of the enterprise. Tools and templates that provide this assistance include the common data matrix, governance activity matrix, communication plan template, questionnaires, and ways to measure the value that is coming from your data governance program.

Enabling Technologies

This type of assistance focuses on leveraging and enabling existing and new technologies that will assist you on the road to formally governing your data. You can use data modeling tools to enforce business definition rules, data dictionary and glossary tools to improve enterprise understanding of data, data quality tools to profile and manage the quality of data in your information systems, and metadata management tools to provide the central hub that is required to make the metadata most useful to your organization. A federated DGO can aid in the consistent and quality implementation of all of the tools that currently, or will exist, in your environment.

Standard Processes and Conventions

This type of assistance includes the facilitation, development, and enforcement of standard data processes that can be used within a business function or across business functions. Standard processes include data quality issue resolution, requests for access to data, and the managed integration of data from different parts of the organization. Conventions include naming conventions, definition conventions, standard use of business objects, and the rules to protect sensitive data. It is the responsibility of the DGO to document, record, and share standards, standard processes, and conventions.

Organizational Policy and Guidelines

This type of assistance ensures that the proper levels of policies and guidelines are in place and made available to support the enforcement of authority over the data. Governance policies and guidelines often focus on regulatory compliance, protecting sensitive data, and sharing data to improve effective use. The DGO or similar central body can provide templates for new policy, process for gaining approval of policy, assurance of access to policy, and assurance that the policies are communicated effectively across the enterprise.

Communication Planning and Delivery

This type of assistance includes developing a communications plan that addresses the business and technical interests of the enterprise. Typical communication plans ensure that there is an appropriate level of orientation to data governance, onboarding of people actively involved in processes associated with governing data, and on-going communications focused on delivering successful governance to all levels of the enterprise. The central body or DGO typically takes on the responsibility for providing consistent and quality communications about data governance across the enterprise.

Business Glossary and Metadata Management

This type of assistance includes the delivery of business glossaries, data dictionaries, and data catalogs, depending on the needs and requirements for managing the metadata associated with their most critical data. This type of assistance focuses on helping the organization to improve its understanding, linkage, and lineage of the data from a cross-enterprise perspective. Organizations focus on business glossaries, data dictionaries, and/or metadata repositories, depending on their needs and requirements for managing the metadata associated with their most critical data. The DGO is often at the heart of developing and delivering the strategy, approach, and implementation of tools associated with governing data as an enterprise asset.

Key Messages

This essay describes the reasons why organizations select to follow the federated model of implementing data governance programs. The essay shares several types of assistance that a federated Data Governance Office (DGO) can provide to the organization. This model provides a high-level of value to organizations that focus on offering standards and guidance while building a strong basis of "self-governance" .

Perspective: Who Should Own Data Governance?

One of the first steps organizations take when preparing to deliver a data governance program is determining where to place data governance within the organization. In other words, determining who should own data governance. I mentioned program ownership earlier in the book as one of the common challenges facing organizations just starting. Figuring out where data governance should live is an important question that every organization must address.

There are typically two common schools of thought: Data governance should either reside in "the business" or IT (Information Technology). I answer the question of who should own data governance with a simple one-word reply. My answer is "Yes." The responsibility to administer or lead data governance must reside somewhere.

Let's answer the questions of where data governance should reside in your organization and who should ensure a program is successful. The typical answer is that the business should own the discipline. This answer is very vague. Are we talking about the financial part of the business or the risk management part of the business? Are we talking about the operations part of the business or the marketing and sales part of the business? There are many facets to the business. Maybe we should be more specific.

---

*The responsibility to administer or lead data governance
must reside somewhere.*

Many organizations position data governance under the Chief Data Officer (CDO), Chief Data and Analytics Officer (CDAO), or Chief Financial Officer (CFO). Other organizations position data governance under the Chief Risk Officer (CRO) or the Chief Operational Officer (COO). In addition, some organizations position data governance under the Chief Privacy Officer (CPO) or the Chief Information Security Officer (CISO). These days there are many C-levels.

The placement of data governance under any one of these C-level people is never wrong. Data governance must reside somewhere, and having a C-level person as your executive sponsor is always good. In fact, many organizations state that senior leadership's support, sponsorship, and understanding of data governance is the number one best practice for starting and sustaining their program. Having a C-level person as your executive sponsor often dictates where data governance will reside in the organization.

The correct placement of your data governance program depends on the ability of that part of the organization to provide the proper capacity in terms of resources to operationalize and engage the organization. No single area of the business deserves to always own data governance. The correct part of the organization is any part that understands the need for data governance and who will support and sponsor the activities of the individuals or groups responsible for administering the data governance program.

Having a C-level person as your executive sponsor is always good.

Data governance programs that do not reside in a business area often reside in IT or under a Chief Data Officer or Office (CDO). The CDO occasionally reports into the Chief Information Officer (CIO). Sometimes the CDO stands alone and sometimes the CDO goes under the name of the Chief Data and Analytics Officer. The positioning of the data governance program sometimes influences where the CDO resides.

Some industry experts claim that the program will fail if data governance is positioned in IT or under the CIO. I am not one of those people. I have seen several organizations demonstrate success with their programs under the top guidance of the CIO. These programs share a trait that data governance is not in place *for* IT's purpose or with IT as the sole owner or steward of the data. Data governance must be a shared responsibility of business people with business knowledge of the data and technical people with technical knowledge of the data, information systems, and data resources. Some industry thought leaders state that data governance fits under a Chief Analytics Officer (CAO). This makes sense for some organizations. However, today only a limited number of organizations formally have a person in the CAO role.

No matter where your data governance resides in your organization, it is a best practice that a person or a group of people in that part of the organization administer the program. If it is a group of people, they are often called the *data governance office* or *data governance team*.

Many organizations initiate their program with a single person responsible for directing the data governance activities. However, some organizations struggle to provide the single person and make administering the program a percentage of a single person's responsibility.

In most cases, a resource dedicated to managing the program is necessary to demonstrate to the organization that management is committed to moving data governance forward. In most cases, a resource is necessary to provide ample attention to gaining requirements, designing, and developing the program, and incrementally rolling the program out into the organization. Experience has shown that many organizations will not add people, and thus capacity, to the running of the program until the strategic level believes that the program is heading in the right direction and that the approach is well thought-out and supported.

The role name often given to the person responsible for the data governance program is the Data Governance Manager, Data Governance Lead, or Data Governance Administrator. This role is typically responsible for managing all organization-wide data governance activities, including partnerships with other governing functions. The role is responsible for reporting the results and status of the program to the strategic level. The position focuses on establishing and ensuring adherence to an enterprise data governance framework for data policies, standards, and practices, both at the enterprise and business function level, to achieve the required level of data quality, data protection, and data availability to meet overall business needs.

Key Messages

The person that leads the data governance program often serves as a point of contact and point of escalation for governance, data quality, and data availability issues. This person works closely with business and functional leadership to improve the availability and value of core data assets and respond to operational, tactical, and strategic requirements.

The program is not owned by a person or a single business unit. The term "owner" implies singular focus and possession of the execution of the program. The organization owns the program. However, as indicated in this essay, the placement of the program and the role of administering the program, plays a critical role in demonstrating value from the data governance program.

Perspective: There is Only One Data Governance

I know that some people will disagree with me. Maybe you believe in master data governance, information governance, metadata governance, big data governance, customer [or insert domain name here] data governance, or data governance 1.0, 2.0, 3.0, or 10.0. But there is only one data governance. And data governance is the execution and enforcement of authority over the management of data and data-related assets.

I am not talking about your organization's approach to implementing data governance. We know the command-and-control, traditional, and non-invasive approaches to data governance described in the earlier essay, *Comparing Approaches to Data Governance*.

Data governance is the execution and enforcement of authority over the management of data and data-related assets.

Data governance 2.0 focuses on how the discipline of data governance is expanding and evolving compared to how we got started in the field. Future versions of data governance highlight our disappointment in how past data governance efforts have failed to deliver on expectations. Newer "versions" expand the breadth of governance to address next-generation data and technologies. The future generations of data governance correct the problems of our past and address future opportunities. However, they still focus on executing and enforcing authority over the management of the data because there is only one data governance.

Master data has been an important data management discipline for years. Think back to when master data became a discussed discipline. Everyone spoke about how important it was to govern our master data. Data governance and MDM became inseparable or connected, leading to the use of the expression "master data governance"—something different from plain old "data governance". Back when big data was new, people recognized the need to govern big data. Big data governance is no different than plain old data governance.

What is next? Smart data governance, unstructured data governance, or audio and video data governance? These names for data governance are nonsense. We do not have to label data governance with these markers because the result of data governance is governed data.

We can discuss data stewardship the same way. Data Stewards are people who are held formally accountable for defining, producing, and using data. That data can be master data, information, metadata, big data—pick a label. If somebody defines, produces, and uses the data related to that label, and they are held formally accountable for how they define, produce, and use the data, then they are a data steward, no matter how you label your data governance effort.

Key Messages

Just like other flavors of governance, metadata governance focuses on the governance of the data about data, or data documentation. Metadata and data are different just like master data and big data are different. But the results of governing the data need to be the same. We need to execute and enforce authority over the management of data and data-related assets.

There is only one data governance.

Perspective: The Same Difference of Data Governance and Data Management

What does your head do when someone uses the expression "same difference"? Mine explodes! Does it mean things are the same? Does it mean there is a difference? Please don't use that expression. It is very confusing. As a matter of language, "same difference" is an idiom—a phrase used in casual conversation to express a speaker's belief that two or more things are essentially the same despite apparent differences.

My consulting experiences reinforce that there is significant confusion about the similarities and differences between data governance and data management and the functions of the same name within organizations. There is no standard or single correct way to organize or address the two disciplines. Organizations need both disciplines, even if that means they are directed by or carried out by different people.

Let's start with familiar and simple definitions of data governance and data management.

Data governance is all about people, their accountability, and their behavior with data. My definition of data governance is "the execution and enforcement of authority over the definition, production, and use of data." Some may say that the "definition, production, and use of data" is the management of data. Data governance focuses on what I refer to at the end of the first Non-Invasive Data Governance book as the Bill of "Rights" (notice the quotes). Data governance is all about getting the "right" people with the "right" knowledge working with the "right" data in the "right" way at the "right" time resulting in the "right" decision.

It takes effort to achieve all of these "rights." There is effort associated with getting each of the core components of the Data Governance Framework "right" for your organization. The components, as I mentioned earlier, include data, roles, processes, communications, metrics, and tools. Data governance work involves metadata management and the administration of the data catalog. The work includes policy, guidelines, standards, ownership, and stewardship of data.

The work efforts of data governance aim to get people to behave more formally and appropriately, leading to consistency and improved value from data.

Data governance is all about the people. We often call these people data stewards—people who define, produce, and use data as part of their job and are held formally accountable for their relationship to the data. I often mention that "everybody is a data steward" if they are held formally accountable for their relationships with the data. Data governance has always been the execution and enforcement of authority, with data stewardship formalizing accountability. These items are all about the people.

In a typical organization, data governance activities may include:

- The execution and enforcement of authority over data.
- The deployment of an operating model of roles & responsibilities for data.
- Data stewardship—formal accountability for data
- Data policies and governing procedures
- Data documentation—glossary, dictionary, catalog
- Behavioral facets of:
    o Metadata
    o Data quality
    o Data taxonomy
    o Data literacy
    o Data processes
    o Legal and compliance

Do any of these areas fall under data management too? That depends on how you define data management.

Dataversity defines data management as a comprehensive collection of practices, concepts, and processes dedicated to leveraging data assets for business success and compliance with data regulations. Data management spans the entire lifecycle of a given data asset from its original creation point to its final retirement, from end to end of an enterprise.[16]

IBM once stated that data management is the practice of ingesting, processing, securing, and storing an organization's data. It is then utilized for strategic decision-making to improve business outcomes.[17]

Both definitions state that data management focuses on delivering practices and processes targeted at successful business outcomes. Data management contains sub-disciplines that vary in number depending on framework. The DAMA Wheel has 10-11 knowledge areas (depending on the version). The CMMI Data Management Maturity framework has five core areas. The EDM Council DCAM framework has eight areas. Typical areas overlapping across these frameworks include data architecture, data quality, metadata management, data operations, and of course, data governance (as the behavioral aspect of data management).

In a typical organization, data management may include the delivery of:

- Data modeling and data architecture platforms
- Data warehousing, business intelligence, and analytical platforms
- Metadata management platforms
- Data quality assurance
- Master data management
- Data transformation, both digital and business
- External data and data ingestion
- Data marketplace, reporting, and visualization

The fact that data governance is called out specifically within each of the popular data management frameworks demonstrates that DAMA International, the CMM Institute, and the EDM Council find it necessary to separate the disciplines of data management and data governance. It may be fair to say that data governance

---

[16] https://www.dataversity.net/what-is-data-management/.

[17] https://www.ibm.com/topics/data-management.

is a subject area of a data management framework and strategy, at least according to these frameworks. But think twice before you say that they are the same thing.

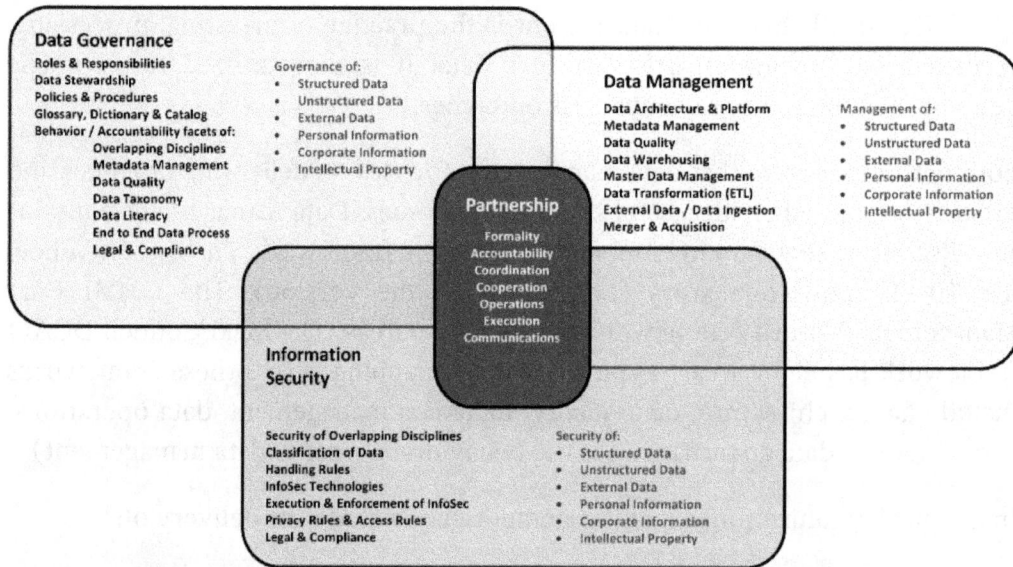

Data Governance

Roles & Responsibilities
Data Stewardship
Policies & Procedures
Glossary, Dictionary & Catalog
Behavior / Accountability facets of:
　　Overlapping Disciplines
　　Metadata Management
　　Data Quality
　　Data Taxonomy
　　Data Literacy
　　End to End Data Process
　　Legal & Compliance

Governance of:
• Structured Data
• Unstructured Data
• External Data
• Personal Information
• Corporate Information
• Intellectual Property

Partnership

Formality
Accountability
Coordination
Cooperation
Operations
Execution
Communications

Data Management

Data Architecture & Platform
Metadata Management
Data Quality
Data Warehousing
Master Data Management
Data Transformation (ETL)
External Data / Data Ingestion
Merger & Acquisition

Management of:
• Structured Data
• Unstructured Data
• External Data
• Personal Information
• Corporate Information
• Intellectual Property

Information Security

Security of Overlapping Disciplines
Classification of Data
Handling Rules
InfoSec Technologies
Execution & Enforcement of InfoSec
Privacy Rules & Access Rules
Legal & Compliance

Security of:
• Structured Data
• Unstructured Data
• External Data
• Personal Information
• Corporate Information
• Intellectual Property

Figure 3-1. Partnership Between Data Governance, Data Management, and Information Security

I recently assisted a client in describing the differences and similarities (the same differences) between data governance and data management for their respective team leaders. The resulting diagram in Figure 3-1 demonstrates that the overlap in these disciplines focuses on partnership in terms of formality, accountability, process, coordination, and communication. Data governance focuses on the people. Data management focuses on the delivery of information technology-based outcomes. Information security (requested by my client) focuses on protecting sensitive information.

All three disciplines, with their overlapping partnership, are set up to incrementally focus on several types of data throughout the organization, including:

• Structured data—typical data governance

• Unstructured data—records and content management

• External data—acquired data

- Personal information—classified and handled
- Corporate—operational data
- Intellectual property—organization-protected data

Key Messages

All three disciplines overlap because they are required to work in harmony with each other. If your organization is presently confused about "who does what" when it comes to how the disciplines of data governance and data management overlap, perhaps, separating them into 1) the people and behavioral activities and 2) the delivery of successful business outcomes through architecture, platforms, and data solutions is a simple way to view the same differences between the two.

CHAPTER 6

Roles as the Program Backbone

E very effective data governance program includes a detailed set of roles and responsibilities. From senior leadership to the strategic, tactical, operational, and support levels of the organization, everybody must understand their responsibilities when it comes to governing data. The data stewards must recognize that how they define, produce, and use data influences the quality of the data and the levels of confidence and trust people have in the data.

This chapter includes an updated version of the roles and responsibilities shared in the first Non-Invasive Data Governance book. In addition, this chapter includes several essays that focus on the essence of data stewardship, how to recognize people as data stewards, guidelines for being a data steward, and why data stewards deserve a raise. The role of the Data Governance Manager is defined in an essay at the end of the chapter.

Experience: Data Governance Roles and Responsibilities

Roles and responsibilities are the backbone of a successful data governance program. Operating an efficient and effective program and holding people formally accountable for how they govern data requires defining and deploying roles that are appropriate for the organization's culture. Communicating effectively with people at all levels of the organization requires roles that represent and address your organization's existing structure. Formalizing accountability for how people define, produce, and use data requires a solid role-based foundation.

This essay covers an updated (since the first book) list of roles and responsibilities to consider at each level of the organization. I refer to the model shown in Figure 3-2 as the Data Governance Operating Model of Roles and Responsibilities.

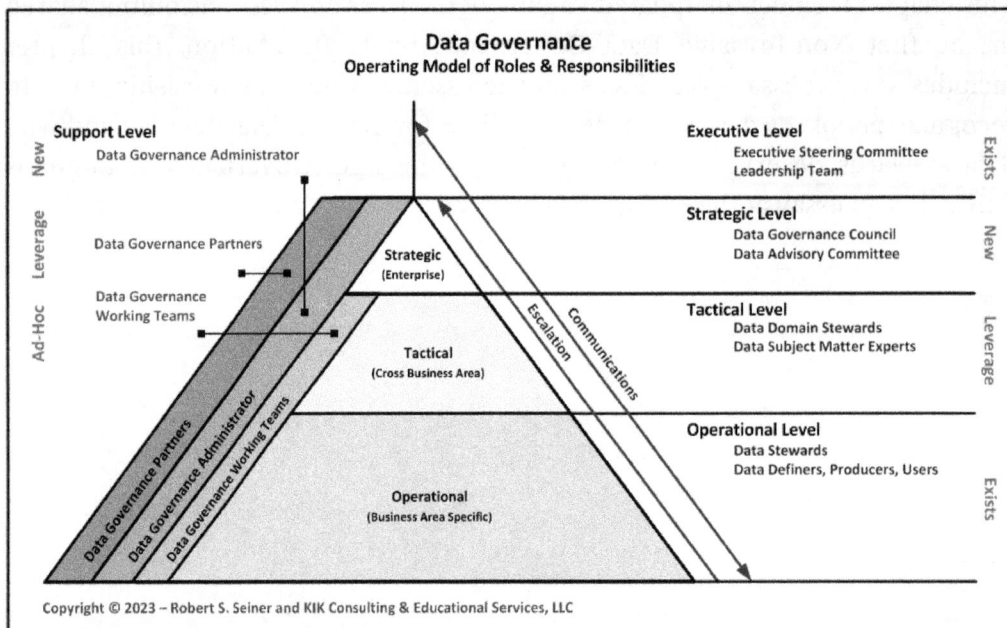

Figure 3-2. Data Governance Roles and Responsibilities

Reading the Operating Model

The Operating Model provides the levels of authority that typically exist within an organization. These levels include the executive, strategic, tactical, operational, and support levels. The operating model you build for your organization should represent the levels that already exist in your organization.

Working from bottom to top of the pyramid, the operational level represents the specific business units or functions of the organization and does not consider cross-business unit decision-making at this level. The next level up, the tactical level, governs data as a cross-business unit resource, effectively breaking down the silos between business units. The strategic level represents the highest level of business unit decision-making, while the executive level is there to guide and steer the organization. It is appropriate to adjust the names of the roles associated with each level based on organizational culture and the appropriate context of data governance. For example, the organization might use the term *"owner"* differently and, therefore, avoid using the word *"owner"* in this model.

The space inside each level of the pyramid represents the estimated percentage of decisions made about the data at this level. Decisions should be made at the operational level if the decisions only affect that level of the organization. This means that most of the decisions will be made within the business units that make up the operation level of the pyramid. Therefore, the amount of space within the operational level of the pyramid is greater than the tactical or strategic levels.

When data decisions impact multiple business units or functions, these decisions are made at the tactical or strategic levels of the model. This will depend on who has the authority to make decisions for the enterprise regarding a certain subject area or domain of data. An example of a domain could be customer data, product data, employee or financial data, or subsets of these domains or subject areas.

Some organizations find it challenging to recognize people in tactical cross-functional roles of their data governance program while other organizations find it easy to recognize the people that already have that responsibility. At the cross-business unit level, the silos of data are broken down, shared, and extracted across business units. Finding the appropriate people to fill the roles associated with decision-making for a specific subject matter of data is not easy. Sometimes this role is pre-defined through policy. Other times, this role is dictated from the highest level of the organization. When the strategic level does not indicate who the tactical steward is, the role is typically filled by someone who volunteers to play the role of facilitator across business units and has no decision-making authority.

When this "volunteer" scenario becomes the case, data issues tend to escalate to the strategic level more regularly. Note the arrows along the right side of the pyramid. One arrow represents a decision-making escalation path from the operational (business function) to strategic (enterprise) authority. The other arrow represents the need for effective communications at and between all levels and roles of the operating model.

The escalation path does not extend to the executive level because data issues are not typically escalated to the senior-most management of an organization. For this reason, the executive level has no space within the pyramid. In my experience, organizations prefer that only five to ten percent of all decision-making be raised to the strategic level. Higher percentages often reflect a lack of authority or facilitation at the tactical level of the organization.

Along the left side of the pyramid are three important roles associated with managing and supporting the program. These include:

- Data Governance Manager, Administrator, Lead or Office – The person or people who have responsibility for managing and administering the program.

- Data Governance Partners – Existing governing functions such as IT, security, risk management, project management, audit, and legal. In addition, some organizations have included business support functions like marketing, communications, project management, change management, and human resources management as partners or support functions of data governance.

- Data Governance Working Teams – Groups of people, typically at the operational and tactical levels of the pyramid, that are brought together to complete a specific action, correct a data problem or address an opportunity to improve the data.

The arrows to the right of the triangle represent:

- The bi-directional data governance communications across all levels of the program.

- A data governance issue escalation path from *operational level* (issues pertains to a single business unit) to *tactical level* (where data is viewed as a multi-business unit resource) to *strategic level* (where the strategic decision is made).

The bullets below provide an updated (since the first book) set of responsibilities associated with each role during program planning and ongoing program deployment.

Executive Level

The responsibilities of a Steering Committee may include:

- Support the data governance program by attending meetings on the subject.

- Communicating to their part of the organization the importance and requirement of formally governing and stewarding data as a valued asset.

- Demonstrating through action (including participating in meetings and providing feedback on activities, active support, and sponsorship) the importance and priority of data governance.

- Sponsor the data governance program by allocating appropriate resources toward the development and sustainability of the program.

- Maintain representation of the corporate business functions and departments on the Data Governance Council.

- Understand the relationships between the data governance program and the results of governed data.

- Include the topic of data governance on the agenda of existing meetings.

- Stay informed about the activities of the Data Governance Manager and program.

- Review and understand data governance success metrics, such as the business value being demonstrated through formal governance practices and the organization's acceptance of the governance program.

- Make program decisions based on Data Governance Manager recommendations, Council recommendations, and program results.

- Approval for the Data Strategy roadmap and its funding (wherever this strategy is developed in the company).

Strategic Level

The responsibilities of a Data Governance Council may include:

- Provide to the Executive Sponsor success stories of value add, status of present activities, assistance necessary to address program issues, deployment of appropriate resources, and understand the steps to take to deliver a successful program.

- Attend regularly scheduled monthly meetings to represent business functions and departments to understand and align data governance activities with corporate and department strategies.

- Communicate to respective Vice Presidents and department leaders the strategic direction and prioritization of data projects to be addressed by Data Governance Working Teams.

- Sponsor data projects focused on improving organizational efficiency and effectiveness and leveraging data to provide competitive advantage.

- Review and approve data policy (including data governance, data ownership, data operational policy) associated with governance before delivering the policy to the Steering Committee for signature.

- Monitor and review Working Team and data project initiatives and status.

- Make decisions to resolve data quality, data opportunity (to address enhancements, enablement, and empowering of staff), and data governance program issues that are escalated to the tactical level by the Data Subject Matter Stewards and Data Governance Working Teams.

- Prioritize data opportunities and submit requests to Data Domain Stewards and the Data Governance Manager to improve the governance of data.

- Be an advocate for change and continuous improvement when it comes to managing data as an asset.

Tactical Level

The responsibilities of the Data Domain Stewards may include:

- Provide subject matter expertise to guide the data solutions focused on achieving quality data in their specific Data Subject Area.

- Establish procedures to formalize the way the organization defines, produces, and uses data as a valued asset.

- Provide subject matter expertise to guide the data solutions focused on achieving quality data in their specific Data Subject Area.

- Participate in facilitating Data Governance Working Team efforts with the Data Governance Manager to achieve quality data in their specific subject matter of expertise.

- Participate as subject matter experts and authoritative representatives on Data Governance Working Teams to improve data definition, production, and usage of strategic data through focused data projects.

- Participate in or fully delegate the collection and development of data documentation and job-aid (and other education/communication materials) associated with data in their specific subject matter of expertise.

- Provide input on in-flight quality data improvement initiatives as needed.

- Be an advocate for the change and continuous improvement when it comes to data as an asset, by effectively communicating benefits and value of a data-driven culture to their part of the organization.

- Responsible for the meaning and the correct usage of data.

- Become educated and lead the operational data stewards in adopting data governance best practices.

Operational Level

The responsibilities of the Operational Data Stewards may include:

- These are people within business functions and departments that are on the front line of data quality issues.

- Responsible for following consistent behaviors when it comes to the defining, producing, and using data.

- Raise awareness of data definition and data usage issues and methods for achieving governed data to the Data Governance Manager through formal channels.

- Operational Data Stewards become educated about data governance by attending meetings, training sessions, industry conferences, and webinars based on their interests.

- Providing appropriate insight into the definition, production, and usage of data, in defining the quality data processes and methods.

- Become formally educated in the data production rules associated with achieving quality data.

- Be an advocate for change and continuous improvement when it comes to data as an asset, by effectively communicating benefits and value of a data-driven culture to their part of the organization.

- Participate as necessary on Data Governance Working Teams to achieve quality data.

- Define and administer system data quality rules.

Support Level

The responsibilities of the Data Governance Manager may include:

- Promote and educate the organizational department business functions about quality data, the Data Governance Program, and its activities and benefits.

- Align the data governance use of technology to the enterprise information strategy.

- Provide strategic advice to the Data Governance Council and follow their guidance and priorities to activate Data Governance Working Teams to achieve quality data.

- Along with Data Subject Matter Stewards and Data Governance Partners, author standards, policies, and procedures in collaboration with business functions and departments. Create reusable DG toolkit, how-to guides.

- Develop, review, and monitor quality data and data governance metrics to assess performance and effectiveness of the data governance program.

- Mentor and consult the Data Governance Council, Data Subject Matter Stewards, Operational Data Stewards, and Working Teams on the Data Governance Program and related Policies, Procedures, and Standards.

- Manages data governance activities and is responsible for reporting the results and status of the quality data effort to the Data Governance Council and Steering Committee.

- Establish and ensure adherence to the enterprise data governance framework for data policies, standards, and practices, both at the enterprise and department business function level, to achieve the required level of data quality and availability of data to meet overall business needs.

- Serve as a point of escalation for governance, data quality, and availability issues. Work closely with business and functional leadership to improve the availability and value of core data assets, respond to operational requirements, and support strategic requirements.

- Works with data governance working teams to improve data quality by defining and using data quality rules.

The responsibilities of the Data Governance Partners may include:

- Provide business and technical advisory support for data governance activities and become actively engaged as needed in providing their expertise.

- Ensure that data documentation critical to improving data quality data and confidence in the data is included in projects and other data-focused activities.

- Existing functional areas that participate in the governance of data. Examples include:

  - *IT*: Secures infrastructure on behalf of organizational departments. Provides technical assistance to the implementation of the data documentation platform.

  - *Legal*: Draft, review, and formalize policy.

  - *Audit*: Responsible for ensuring auditable compliance with laws and regulations.

  - *Human Resources:* Direct efforts to include governance responsibilities in job descriptions.

  - *Corporate Communications*: Provide guidance and assistance in data governance messaging, including adjusting content to address specific audiences and roles.

- Responsible for supporting the integration of data governance within the standard project methodology.

- Ensure that standard project methodology is followed and that policies, procedures, and metrics are in place for maintaining/improving data quality and creating, capturing, and maintaining data documentation.

- Provide technical support for quality data and data governance efforts when required.

The responsibilities of the Data Governance Working Teams may include:

- Facilitated by the Data Governance Manager to address quality data issues or participate in data projects.

Working groups should be formed and engaged to:

- Improve enterprise data definitions and standards for critical data elements (CDE).

- Improve data production and collection.

- Improve data usage and understanding of business data rules.

- Improve data quality through data documentation and metadata.

Key Messages

As stated earlier, roles and responsibilities are the backbone of data governance program success. The core components of a data governance program described earlier in this book must be viewed from the perspective of each of the levels and associated governing roles of the organization.

This essay includes a detailed description of a Data Governance Operating Model of Roles and Responsibilities, how to design a set of roles to imitate your organization's culture, and how to read the model. The essay also shares a list of roles and sample responsibilities to consider at each level of the organization.

Perspective: Data is Everybody's Job

Data governance is all about getting the "right" people to do the "right" thing at the "right" time focused on delivering the "right" results. I referred to this in the first book as being the Data Governance Bill of "Rights".

Formal accountability for data is my definition of data stewardship. Organizations face the challenge of getting people to do the right thing because either they do not know what the right thing is to do or they are not formally being held accountable for doing the right thing.

Formal accountability for data is my definition of data stewardship.

What happens when people who should be accountable for producing quality data as part of their job clearly want nothing to do with producing data? What happens when these people say, "It's not my job," and act accordingly? What happens when the data they should produce can improve operations, marketing, sales, or engineering? Does the organization allow them to get away with refusing to produce high-quality data? What is the best way to deal with these people who say that it is not their job to produce the data?

I have stated often in this and the last book that "everybody is a data steward" and the organization must "get over this fact." To cover the entire organization with governance and stewardship of data, everybody with a relationship to data must be held accountable for that relationship. The relationships are as definers, producers, or users of that data.

Let's use as an example an organization that wants to improve the trust, confidence, understanding and value people get from the data. In that case, people who define data must be held accountable for how they define the data. This accountability can include checking whether or not data with the same definition already exists before creating new data. This accountability can include re-using existing data whenever possible. This can include the responsibility for providing strong business definitions for the data. The definition of the data will not improve by itself, and providing standards for how the data is defined will typically lead to improvements in the consistency and completeness of data definitions.

The definition of data will not improve itself.
Providing standards for data definition leads to improved definitions.

People who use data must be held formally accountable for how they use data. Everybody that uses sensitive data must be held formally accountable for protecting that data. That is what the law says and the government will hold you accountable. Many data governance or data security programs are put in place to protect sensitive data.

If people who define data must be held accountable for how they define data, and those who use data must be held accountable for how they use data, where does that leave the people who produce the data? I would guess that you didn't answer that question by thinking, "we let them only produce the data (or the quality of the data) that they want to produce." Instead, people on the front line of producing data must also be held formally accountable for the data they produce.

Salespeople in many organizations are not particularly interested in entering data into systems. The same is true for technical engineers. The salespeople say they are responsible for closing sales. The engineers say that they are responsible for designing and creating product specifications. I have recently worked with two organizations where people have stated that the production of data is not their job leaving nobody to produce the necessary data. Problems can arise from allowing these people to reject the notion that they are responsible for entering data.

It is important to recognize that the ability to close sales often depends on data about prospects, products and services the prospects are buying, and the contacts and transactions that take place every step toward closing the sale. It is also important to recognize that the delivery of well-engineered products requested by customers often depends on the data about specifications, materials, availability, and so much more. If we cannot expect the salespeople and engineers to produce the data, then there has to be an alternative way to get the appropriate data produced in a quality and timely manner.

I see that there are two options to resolve this problem:

1. Require the salespeople and engineers to produce the data. Requiring them to produce the data may be rejected if these people are given the authority to say that data production is not their job. Perhaps if they truly understand how the production of the data will improve not only their performance, but also the performance of the organization, they will see why they are being requested to take on data-focused responsibility. Oftentimes, the amount of time required to produce the data is minimal but would require changing the "way they have always done things."

2. Provide a resource to work with the salespeople and engineers. This person can take on the responsibility of promptly producing the data. This is a non-invasive way to satisfy the same requirement. This does not require an additional resource per salesperson or engineer, but rather, the addition of a data production steward ("person who is responsible for producing data"), who assists and works with the salespeople and engineers. The number of data production steward resources will depend on the number of salespeople and engineers within your organization.

Key Messages

In the cases shared in this essay, either the option of 1) telling the people that they must produce the data (more invasive), or 2) making certain that a resource is available to work with people to produce the data (less invasive), are viable approaches. We cannot choose the option to not produce data. This is especially true when the data in question is critical to improving the operations of the organization.

The same holds true for people who define and use the data. Formal data governance requires that people who define, produce, and use data follow the rules or guideline for how to appropriately take those actions. Data is everybody's job. We all know that the data will not define, produce or use itself.

Perspective: A Steward is a Steward

"A rose by any other name would smell as sweet" is a popular maxim from William Shakespeare's play, Romeo and Juliet, in which Juliet argues that it does not matter that Romeo is from her family's adversary house of Montague. If a rose smells like a rose no matter what you call it, can the same be said about stewards? Not about the smell :), but about what we call these people.

A steward, by definition, is someone who takes care of something for someone else. The people in the organization take care of the organization's data for the organization. A steward is not an "owner." A steward is a caretaker.

A person who defines what data is needed by their part of the organization, defines that data to be consumed by the organization, defines the acceptable level of quality for that data, checks to see if that data already exists before defining it yet another way, is a data definition steward. The data definition steward takes care of the business definition of that data for the organization.

A person in the organization who produces data, and intentionally knows and follows the quality rules and standards associated with producing that data is a data production steward. The data production stewards take care of producing quality data for the organization.

A person who uses data, and intentionally knows and follows the rules and standards associated with how to use that data, are data usage stewards. The data usage steward takes care of how the organization uses data.

The non-invasive approach to data governance considers the idea that becoming a data steward is not something that people can opt-in or opt-out of. A person is a data steward if they have a relationship to the data (as a definer, producer, or user of data) and they are held formally accountable for that relationship and the actions they take with data. The people leading the data governance efforts need to know who those people are. As I have stated earlier in the book, "everybody is a data steward."

Some people consider these people to be operational data stewards or refer to them as data definers, producers, and users. People typically take more than one of these actions with data. It is common that people define and use the data, or they produce and use the data. These people are operational data stewards who are most concerned with doing their respective jobs and often have limited (because of time constraints) interest in doing things that benefit the organization as a whole.

There is a second level of stewardship, often referred to as being tactical. Tactical data stewards are people that take care of, or who are accountable for, subject matters or domains of data that cross organizational boundaries. The distinction between the operational data steward and the tactical data steward lies in the scope of the steward's insights and authority. An operational steward focuses on the data specific to their function, while the tactical steward is concerned with data shared by multiple business functions.

As an example, in a University setting, the registrar may be the tactical data steward for student data wile the bursar is the tactical data steward for financial aid data. The second level of stewardship focuses on the interests of the entire organization and the quality and confidence people have in that data.

The tactical data steward often is referred to as the Data Owner. When organizations use the term "owner," this sends a message that conflicts with the message of becoming a data steward. To remind you, the data steward is formally accountable for taking care of the data for the organization. Using the term "owner" implies exactly the opposite of what stewardship embraces. Ownership declares, "This is mine. I own it. I make the decisions about it." In the non-invasive approach to data governance, we typically refer to the tactical data stewards as the Data Domain (subject matter) Stewards or the Data Subject Matter Experts (DSMEs).

The tactical steward often has the authority or accountability to make decisions for the organization. In the non-invasive approach, the strategic level Data Governance Council has the responsibility to make decisions that get escalated from the tactical to the strategic level of the organization.

Consider the following personal traits when you recognize your tactical level stewards:

- Vision of what the future of that domain of data (as an asset) looks like.

- Looking for ways to improve the status quo for the domain.

- Ability to motivate the organization.

- Set an example of data-related behavior.

- Team player.

- Diplomatic.

- Personal interest, intuitive ability, and communication skills to facilitate issue resolution to achieve a "win-win."

Key Messages

The success of a maintainable data governance program depends on the strength of the operational and tactical data stewards. A data domain steward at the tactical level ensures that the right actions are being taken with the data within that domain or subject area. This can lead to uncomfortable situations where authority and enforcement are unclear.

Data governance is "the execution and enforcement of authority over the definition, production, and usage of data." Rules must be followed. Data must be governed. Stewardship is an important part of successful data governance, especially at the operational and tactical levels.

Perspective: What Makes a Data Steward

Your organization most likely has many people who have access to sensitive data. They must all protect that data. The government (and your customers) will not be happy if only a percentage of these people are accountable for protecting the data. Therefore, everyone who uses sensitive data must protect that data. My experience tells me that you should consider these people to be data (usage) stewards. Everybody is a data steward if they are held formally accountable for how they use the data.

Holding somebody formally accountable for data requires that they know and understand the difference between healthy and unhealthy data-related behavior. And that means that somebody in the organization must be held accountable for defining healthy behavior in terms of people's daily relationships to the data. Practicing formal accountability also means that there must be consequences for not following the standards for data-related behavior. That is what makes the accountability formal.

What about those people in your organization who define the data required for operations, analytics, customer satisfaction, and decision-making? Are they being held accountable for the data they define and what does that mean?

Data definers are those who define data that the organization requires to operate. Data definers create new systems or acquire new packages, applications, or data to benefit the organization. Data definers should be accountable for:

- considering that the data may already exist before defining new data.

- making certain that the data is well-documented, meaning that the appropriate metadata and business rules are documented and available.

- data classification so the people can protect the data per the defined rules.

People who define data are automatically data stewards when held formally accountable for the actions I just mentioned.

What about those people who produce the data required for daily operations? Should they be held accountable for the data they produce and what does that mean?

Data producers are the people on the front lines who enter data into your systems. Data producers acquire data from outside the organization to benefit them in their job function. Data producers are those people that combine, merge, select, and enhance data that already exists to form new data. Data producers are the people that populate the data defined as being necessary to run the business. Data producers should be accountable for:

- understanding how the organization will use the data they produce.

- the quality of the data they produce or enter into the packages or applications.

- the data they bring into the organization from the outside, including the quality, confidence, and protection of that data.

People that produce data are automatically data stewards when held formally accountable for the data they produce.

And what about those in your organization that use the data defined and produced by the people mentioned in the previous paragraphs? Are they being held accountable for how they use the data, and what does that mean?

Data users have access to the data in your information systems and databases. Data users have access to the data for reporting and analytical purposes. Data users should be accountable for how they use data, who they share it with, and how they disseminate it within or outside the organization. Data users should be accountable for:

- knowing the rules associated with using the data.

- protecting the data based on its classification.

- sharing the rules with the people with whom they share data.

People that use data are automatically data stewards when they are held formally accountable for the data they use.

Key Messages

The people that define, produce, and use data in your organization are stewards of the data if they are being held accountable for these actions. Stewards of the data must know and follow healthy data-related behavior. That means that somebody in the organization must define the healthy behavior in terms of people's daily relationships with the data. Practicing formal accountability also means that there must be consequences for not following the standards for data-related behavior. That is what makes accountability formal and makes a person a data steward.

Perspective: Data Stewards Should Get a Raise

Perhaps you thought, by the title of this essay, that I am talking about data stewards deserving more money for what they do. That is not what I meant (but I am all for it). There are other raises that people receive by becoming data stewards. What raise(s) will your data stewards see from becoming a data steward?

To provide credit where credit is due, this article stemmed from a conversation I had with a client. My client is working on onboarding her data stewards. As part of the certification (actually more awareness and literacy) process, she wants to let them know what's in it for them (WIIFT– or WIIFM [me] from the steward perspective).

The act of onboarding data stewards is a common data governance program activity. The following is a list of raises and benefits that can be gained by becoming a data steward:

- Raised profile and voice. Being recognized as a knowledgeable person about data in a specific domain, information system, or across business functions or critical processes brings certain benefits. Having your profile raised by becoming active as a data steward assures that you will be "in the room where it happens" (to steal a line from Hamilton) and consulted when important discussions take place or decisions made.

- Raised literacy and awareness. Accepting the recognition as a data steward often presents the opportunity to increase the levels of data literacy and data awareness. Stewardship communities can provide additional levels of education, training, and mentoring. Being able to tell "stories about data" and "stories with data" increases opportunities for people that accept and adopt the role of data steward.

- Raised efficiency (effectiveness). Data stewards who actively define, produce, and use data, are the "eyes and ears" on people in the best position to inform the organization where ungoverned data cause inefficiencies and ineffectiveness. Time spent wrangling data negatively impacts business analysts, data analysts, and data scientists. Time spent looking for data, requesting access to data, and then clearing hurdles to access the data limit all stewards' ability to work efficiently and effectively. Becoming a data steward raises the individual's ability to highlight deficiencies across the organization.

- Raised job performance. Data stewards who 1) recognize that they are being held formally accountable for the data they define, produce, and use, 2) take the appropriate steps to take care of the data per that accountability for their actions, and 3) are evaluated in part based on how they satisfy that accountability, often out-perform their colleagues who do not meet these three criteria. Formal stewardship plays an instrumental role in the success of a data governance program.

- Raised business results. Inconsistent definitions and uses of data weaken business results. Engaging data stewards where and how they work reduces risk, improves business performance, and improves decision-making.

Key Messages

When stewardship is weak, people who define, produce, and use data as part of their daily job do so without understanding the impact they have on the entire organization. These people are taking actions daily with data without being fully aware, updated, instructed, rehearsed, and held accountable for their actions.

This lack of understanding weakens the organization's business results since it leads to inconsistent definition, production, and usage of data. Engaging data stewards where and how they work reduces risk, and improves business performance and decision-making. These are the true benefits of being a data steward.

Experience: Guidelines for Recognizing Data Stewards

I am often asked, "How do we determine who the appropriate data stewards are in our organization?" I quickly answer this question, "Everybody is a data steward because everyone, at some time, encounters data or uses data as part of their everyday jobs." Formally engaging or providing data awareness to everybody in the organization is not a bad idea. But formally engaging everybody as data stewards in the same exact way is not a good idea. Let me explain with some basic rules.

A Data Steward can be Anybody

If you follow the Non-Invasive Data Governance approach, you may have heard me say that you cannot tag each data steward and say, "You're it" and expect him or her to instantly begin stewarding data. That's not the way it works.

However, every person who defines, produces, and uses data in your organization has a level of accountability or responsibility for how they define, produce, and use data. These levels of accountability are often informal, inefficient, and ineffective when it comes to the necessary levels of accountability that comprise a successful environment for governing your data.

People on the front line are accountable for entering data appropriately and accurately. People who define data have accountability for ensuring they're not redefining something already defined. And certainly, individuals who use data have accountability for how they use data.

Accountability for data is often informal
which leads to inefficiency and ineffectiveness.

This is the main concept of the Non-Invasive Data Governance approach. If we can formalize the accountability of stewards and convince management and the stewards that they are already stewarding informally, this will improve communications. I can already hear data stewards saying, "Do you mean I already do this stuff?" Of course, your response is, "Yes. We want to put some formality around some of the things we already do." And their response is, "Oh, okay, I think I get it now."

Being a Data Steward Describes a Relationship to Data and Not a Position

Being a data steward is neither a position nor a title. Being a data steward describes a relationship between a person and some data, which could be a data element, data set, subject area, application, database—however granular you want to get with your association of steward to data. In the data governance operating model shared earlier, although we distinguished between data definition stewards, data production stewards, and data usage stewards, most organizations don't differentiate among types of operational data stewards.

Those who define data as part of their jobs should have formal accountability for making certain they record and make available a sound business description of the data they define. Or perhaps they should be accountable for identifying and using existing data. Or they should have accountability to get the appropriate people involved in the efforts to define the data.

This person can be associated with Business Intelligence (BI), Customer Relationship Management (CRM), Enterprise Resource Planning (ERP), Master Data Management (MDM), big data, package implementation, or efforts to move your data to the cloud where new data is being defined for an organization. The Non-Invasive Data Governance approach calls for data definition stewards to become formally accountable for data definition quality.

Those who produce data as part of their jobs should have formal accountability for making certain that data is produced and recorded following the business rules. Or perhaps they should be accountable for ensuring that the data they produce is entered into the system in a timely manner. Or they should be accountable for making certain that appropriate people are notified when data is updated, when data accuracy provides low confidence levels, or when data has not been received. This individual can be a data-entry person, a data integrator, a data analyst, a report generator, or a person involved in any of the efforts described in the above paragraph. The Non-Invasive Data Governance approach calls for data-production stewards to become formally accountable for how they produce data.

And this leaves the data-usage stewards. Everyone who uses data in a job should be held accountable for how he, she, or they use that data. This means that the data governance program should focus early on recording and making available the regulatory, compliance, classification, and risk rules associated with data usage. The data-usage steward should be held formally accountable for individuals with whom data is shared. The data usage steward should be accountable for securing and protecting the data according to the recorded and available rules. This person could be anybody in the organization who uses data for their job.

Does this mean we need to physically record every single individual in the organization who has a relationship to data? Well, probably not. Do we need to know every division, department, and group that defines, produces, and uses the data? Probably so. I developed a Common Data Matrix spreadsheet tool that I shared in the first book that I repeatedly use with organizations to help them formally record who does what with specific data across their organizations.

A Data Steward is Not Hired to be a Data Steward

I've seen organizations post Full-Time-Equivalent (FTE) jobs of data stewards. I think this is a mistake for most organizations. As you can tell from my rules thus far, I think data stewards already exist in your organization and can be anybody. I make this a rule because the people in your environment are already the stewards of data even though they may not formally consider themselves as such.

In my Operating Model of Roles and Responsibilities, I differentiate between operational data stewards, described in the previous rule, and data domain stewards at the tactical level. The data domain steward typically has a level of formal accountability or sometimes authority to make decisions for a specific domain or subject area of data for an entire organization or whatever part of the organization falls under the guidance of the data-governance program. The data domain steward is also typically not a position for which an organization hires somebody.

Some organizations designate data domain stewards through formal guidelines and policies. A university I recently worked with focused on data classification as the primary driver of its data-governance program. The classification policy spelled out that the registrar was the data trustee (another name for data domain steward) of student data, that the controller was the trustee of financial data, and the vice president of human resources was the trustee of employee (staff) data. This way of doing things is becoming more typical than we may think.

It makes sense for organizations to spell out the person(s) who are responsible for the data domain steward by position in the organization. In some organizations, this position is not total authority on that subject matter of data. Yet, this person is held in high enough regard across the organization to make certain that the data in their subject matter is governed properly.

When the data domain steward is not the authority or person who can make decisions for the organization, it becomes the responsibility of the data governance council at the strategic level to make these decisions. My experience is that decisions about data rarely escalate from the council to the executive level. So again, the same as the operational data steward, the data domain steward is not a role that someone is hired to fill.

A Data Steward Does Not Need the Title of Data Steward

If everybody is a steward of data, then there's no reason to change people's job titles. Changing people's titles will be complicated, expensive, and confusing. As I stated earlier, a steward can be a person with any title. Therefore, to stay less invasive, we should allow individuals to retain their original titles and educate them on the formal accountabilities accompanying their relationships to data. In most cases, this won't mean a major work shift for data stewards. This does not mean there will be no work shift, but it won't be a redefinition of their position or what they do.

The same holds true for the data domain steward. A controller need not be called the finance data domain steward, and a registrar doesn't have to be called the student data domain steward. It's most important that these individuals are recognized as the persons filling the role of the data domain steward.

A Data Steward Does Not Have to be Told How to do Their Job

People like to discuss whether or not data stewards need to be told how to be data stewards, and whether data stewards can be certified as data stewards. The answer to both considerations is that it depends. What does it depend on?

In my experience, data stewards do not have to be taught how to be data stewards. Rather, data stewards can be educated on the formalities of their existing relationships with data. A person who uses data must be educated on what data means, where data came from, how data may or may not be used, how data may or may not be shared, etc. A person who produces data must be educated on the impact of how data is entered and the guidelines for producing that data. I think you get my point.

In some ways, you could say that data stewards need to be told what this formality means and how to be the best data stewards they can be. Then the question becomes, "Does this mean we need to tell data stewards how to do their jobs?" And to that, I say a resounding, "No." We don't have to teach data stewards how to do their jobs. We just help them to do their jobs more consistently in terms of the data they define, produce, and use.

Public or Industry Data Steward Certification is a Load of Bunk

This is the second half of the answer to the questions raised by the previous rule. I firmly believe that data stewards cannot be certified. Every data steward has a different relationship with data and, therefore, a different responsibility. Some public service or consulting organizations focus on certifying data stewards. I'm against this idea. I am against somebody else certifying your people as data stewards. I am not against a practitioner organization setting up credentials and training internally for their stewards to certify them in their positions as a steward of the specific data they define, produce, and use.

Organization certification, yes. There are well-documented cases of organizations certifying their own data stewards.

Industry certification, no. To have an industry group certify data stewards would be like telling them how to do their jobs. And you already know that this subject is covered by the previous rule.

More Than One Data Steward Exists for Each Type of Data

Many organizations point at individuals and say, "Jim, he is our Customer Data Steward." "Mary, over there, she is our Product Data Steward." "Mike is our Employee Data Steward."

If you refer to people that way, you may want to stop doing that. Identifying people this way is not right. At least not if you follow any of the rules I've outlined above. Please remember that having only one data steward per type, category, or subject matter is not consistent with the Non-Invasive Data Governance approach. That is, unless you are talking about data domain or subject matter stewards who could be given the role of customer data domain steward, product data domain steward, etc. These people have accountability across business areas. Do not forget to insert the word *domain* or *subject area* into the role name to define the role's responsibilities more clearly.

There are multiple data stewards for practically every type of data in your organization if you include every person with a relationship with data. Do we need to know exactly who all these people are and call them data stewards? Do we need to know that there are people with a relationship to a particular type of data within a certain part of an organization? Knowing who the stewards are and knowing where they live in the organization is important to the success of your data governance program.

Data Steward Training Should Focus on Formalizing Accountability

Rather than certifying individuals as data stewards, a data-governance program should focus on educating data stewards in your specific organization about the formal accountabilities of their specific relationships to data. Definers are educated on the accountabilities that go with defining data. Producers are educated on accountabilities that go with data production. Perhaps most important, users receive education on accountabilities related to using data. And individuals who actively have two of the three relationships or three of the three relationships receive data governance education on all relationships that apply to them.

And not just general education about what data stewards do. I'm talking about education that specifically pertains to the definition, production, and use of data *they* use or data *they* steward as part of their everyday jobs. This may be scary for some organizations, since they may not have the accountabilities of each relationship for each type of data defined in a way that can be shared with their data stewards.

Key Messages

This essay covered rules for associating people with the role of the data steward. I continue to share the idea that everybody is a data steward and that stewardship defines a person's relationship to the data rather than something brand new. I suggest that falling short of these stewardship rules will fall short of data governance that covers the entire organization.

Experience: A Data Governance Manager Job Description

From time to time, I get asked to provide a job description for the person who will run an organization's data governance program. My experience is that there are several approaches to data governance, and the approach chosen dictates the type of person you need. My experience also has shown me that the reasons why organizations put data governance programs in place and the size, complexity, and political landscape also can be used to indicate the necessary qualifications, skills, and leadership capabilities for the job.

Therefore, it isn't easy to address every organization's requirement in a single data governance manager's job description that is generic enough to be applied to every organization. I will be general. Use the following job description as a general outline and template to construct your own data governance manager job description.

Job description

- Our organization will require that a data governance manager lead and manage all organization-wide data governance activities and be responsible for improving the quality and protecting sensitive data and information assets. The position will focus on establishing and ensuring adherence to an enterprise data governance framework for data policies, standards, and practices, both at the department and business and functional areas level, to achieve the required level of consistency, quality, and protection to meet overall business needs.

- The data governance manager serves as a point of escalation for governance, data quality, and protection issues and will work closely with business and functional area leadership to improve the quality and value of core data assets, respond to regulatory protection requirements, and support the strategic requirements of the department.

Roles and responsibilities

- Establish and govern an enterprise data governance implementation roadmap, including strategic priorities for developing information-based capabilities.

- Roll out an enterprise-wide data governance framework, focusing on improving data quality and protecting sensitive data through modifications to organization behavior policies and standards, principles, governance metrics, processes, related tools, and data architecture.

- Define roles and responsibilities related to data governance and ensure clear accountability for stewardship of the organization's principal information assets.

- Serve as a liaison between business and functional areas and technology to ensure that data-related business requirements for protecting sensitive data is clearly defined, communicated, understood, and considered as part of operational prioritization and planning.

- Develop and maintain inventory of the enterprise information maps, including authoritative systems and owners.

- Facilitate developing and implementing data quality standards, data protection standards, and adoption requirements across the enterprise.

- Define indicators of performance and quality metrics and ensure compliance with data-related policies, standards, roles and responsibilities, and adoption requirements.

- Lead senior management, comprising resources from the business and functional areas and IT business and operations functions, to achieve their objectives; resolve issues escalated from business and functional areas data governance representatives.

- In conjunction with IT, provide progress reports to board management and oversee periodic updates to the department data governance roadmap.

- Coordinate external data sources to eliminate redundancy and streamline the expense related to those services.

- Identify new business opportunities for using information assets to achieve efficiency and effectiveness in the marketplace/represent data as a strategic business asset at the senior management table.

Qualifications

- Minimum of ___ years of experience in a major services organization with large-scale data or project management and oversight experience. Minimum of ___ years with a major organization.

- ___ years in a senior management role, with board level change or transformation leadership experience.

- Knowledge of industry-leading data quality and data protection management practices.

- Knowledge of data governance practices, business, and technology issues related to the management of enterprise information assets and approaches related to data protection.

- Knowledge of data-related government regulatory requirements and emerging trends and issues.

- Demonstrated consulting skills with change management concepts and strategies, including communication, culture change, and performance measurement system design.

- Knowledge of risk data architecture and technology solutions.

- Internally and externally recognized subject matter expert who can influence how things are done.

- Bachelors or master's in computer science, MIS, or information management.

Desired skills

Leadership

- Highest personal and professional integrity and strong work ethics.

- Ability to articulate vision of transformation efforts and a sense of mission.

- Willingness to take change and provide direction.

- Results orientation, willingness to commit to a direction and drive operations to completion.

- Demonstrated ability to manage adversity and challenging situations.

Relationship management

- Ability to manage senior relationships across all the business and functional areas.

- Ability to develop cooperative and constructive working relationships.

- Ability to handle complaints, settle disputes, resolve conflicts, and negotiate with others.

- Collaborative team player orientation towards work relationships, strong culture awareness.

Project oversight and decisioning

- Highly developed skills in priority setting and alignment of project priorities with departmental strategy.

- Ability to break down complex problems and projects into manageable goals.

- Ability to get to the heart of the problem and make sound and timely decisions to resolve problems.

People management and development

- Ability to develop people, coaching, mentoring, and teaching skills on the job.

- Ability to identify and recruit talent, including identifying the right people for both technical and non-technical jobs.

- Skills at performance management, recognizing and rewarding performance, and identifying development needs.

- Effectiveness in building trust, respect, and cooperation among teams.

Key Messages

The role of the Data Governance Manager or Program Administrator is critical to the success of your program. The manager is the person responsible for defining and guiding the core activities of the program including arranging for foundational components, communicating with leadership and stakeholders, operationalizing the program, and engaging the data stewards. This essay shares a basic description of the role and desired skills of the Data Governance Manager.

Experience: The Key Role of the Data Governance Partner

Data governance partners are existing functions in the organization that already govern. They may not be formally labeled as governance functions. For example, the human resources function already governs the activities of employees and staff. The legal function already governs the lawful matters of the organization. The Project Management Office (PMO) already governs the activities of projects. Functions like these do not have to be labeled as "governance," but they all focus on executing and enforcing authority over something.

The existing levels of governance performed by these functions do not have to be replicated by the data governance function. And these functions do not need to replicate the function of data governance. Sounds simple enough. In fact, the existing levels of accountability held by these functions can be leveraged as part of your data governance program if your mission is to stay non-invasive in your approach.

Examples of data governance partners include:

- Information Technology (IT)
- Information Security
- Internal Audit/Legal
- Human Resources
- Finance
- Corporate Communications
- Project Management Office (PMO)
- Change Management Office (CMO)

Let's begin by focusing on the role of the data governance partner and how each example shared above can already be considered partners of your data governance program.

Description of Data Governance Partner Role

The role of the data governance partner is literally to do their job function. This sounds simple and understated, but the truth is that this modest fact lies at the heart of the role of the data governance partner. The data governance partner already has a function not dictated by the data governance program. However, the actions taken by the partners in their regular function can benefit from implementing effective governance.

And the opposite is also true. The partner functions can often directly benefit from working with the data governance program. Let's walk through each of the data governance partner examples I shared above.

From my experience, the following departments participate in data governance programs in the role of the data governance partner:

Information Technology (IT)

The Information Technology department is considered to be a most important partner of the data governance program. In fact, from time-to-time, you will see the program reside in IT. Some pundits will tell you that a data governance program located within IT will always fail. I am not one of those pundits.

When asked if data governance should reside in IT or in a business area, my answer is always "Yes." Your program needs to reside somewhere. Programs in IT that focus on data solely for IT's purposes are destined to fail. Programs that focus on the needs of the business can reside anywhere in the organization. The same holds true for data management.

The role of IT is to do their job. The roles of the data architect and the data modeler are very important when it comes to the technical governance of the data architecture and the governed definition of modeled data. The architects and modelers are likely the IT roles that are most focused on the organization's data.

Successful IT operations are important to the success of a data governance program. The data governance function should leverage the fact that IT already has a set of responsibilities that are not dictated by the data governance program. IT is the most important data governance partner of this set. Organizations that do not leverage IT knowledge, expertise, and management to further their program are doing themselves a great disservice.

Information Security

Information Security is a governing practice of protecting data and information by mitigating risks. Information security is often a part of a greater information risk management function and typically governs against unauthorized or inappropriate access to data. This function focuses on executing and enforcing authority over data access by setting guidelines for who can access the data and granting authority to those individuals and groups. Through its function, information security records and manages all activities, and records a significant amount of information (metadata) about who has access to what.

The data governance program also wants to know who can access the data. Data governance is also interested in formalizing the person accountable for classifying the data. Data governance is actively involved with documenting and formalizing the responsibilities of the person granting permission for people and groups to access the data. Data governance takes a keen interest in ensuring that the people who work with sensitive data know the rules for handling and securing the data.

The interests of information security and data governance overlap. These functions are partners that can benefit greatly by communicating effectively and leveraging each other's knowledge and experience. Information security plays the role of a partner in successful data governance programs.

Internal Audit/Legal

The internal audit and legal departments can certainly be partners of your data governance program. I have been known to say that the auditors are friends of the data governance program only to be shut down by people that make fun of that statement (maybe they do not realize that I am speaking about internal auditors). An internal audit aims to examine finances and provide management controls systematically, purposefully, and independently. People auditing from inside the organization typically understand what external auditors will be "looking for" when they investigate your organization.

When engaged as a partner of your program, an internal audit function can provide an unbiased opinion of the data governance program's strengths and weaknesses. Working with your internal audit function can help your data governance program proactively avoid rather than react to issues. Internal auditors are good data governance partners.

Data governance partners already have a function which is not dictated by the data governance program.

The legal department may also be a partner of your data governance program. The legal function is typically responsible for reviewing and approving contracts, policies, purchase agreements, and other important documents. The legal function can also influence other aspects of the program, including roles and responsibilities, charters, and plans, and members of the legal department may also participate at the strategic level of the program (data governance council).

Legal and internal auditors must be considered data governance partners.

Human Resources

The Human Resources (HR) department governs aspects of employment, such as compliance with labor law and employment standards, interviewing, and administration of employee benefits. Human resources is typically accountable for organizing employee data and most aspects of recruitment and termination. The HR department serves as the link between an organization's management and its employees.

Human resources has a relationship to the data governance program in several ways. HR staff are stakeholders and stewards of critical data that must be protected. HR's data must be of high quality and documented to enable the department to analyze and assess how to improve employee relations and bring out the best work ethic of the employees.

Just like HR, the data governance function is all about the organization's people and getting them to behave appropriately when defining, producing, and using data. I define data governance as "the execution and enforcement of authority over the management of data" and data stewardship as "the formalization of accountability for the management of data." These definitions are people-centric as governance stresses that employees are expected to follow rules and guided or standardized behavior. Failure to follow the rules brings consequences. The HR department will most likely be involved in any disciplinary action an organization takes against its employees due to a lack of governance and stewardship.

Human resources may not be the first group you think of when trying to identify your data governance partners. However, the HR department is key in all things employee-related, and data governance directly impacts employees.

Finance

Your organization's finance department plays an important role as they govern all matters about managing, creating, and studying money and investments. Finance governs the use of monetary resources and the actions that managers take to increase the value of the organization to the stakeholders and shareholders. Finance's actions must abide by their industry's compliance and regulatory rules, and the finance department typically manages reporting and auditability. Finance, most likely, was one of the first parts of the organization to formally govern data as finance departments were one of the earliest adopters of data governance best practices.

Although not all organizations make the same choices, the Chief Financial Officer (CFO) is often the data governance program's executive sponsor (ultimately accountable for the program's success). Other C-level positions that often sponsor data governance programs include CDOs (data), CIOs (information), CRO (risk), and COO (operations).

Whether the CFO is your data governance executive sponsor or not, financial compliance and regulatory controls require governance. Reporting and auditability require governance. People in finance are stakeholders and stewards of critical data and are often the first people in the organization to recognize the importance of formal governance.

Corporate Communications

Your Corporate Communications group is an important partner to your data governance program. This group is often overlooked as a partner but must be considered for the value it can bring to your program. In terms of data governance, communications specialists can focus on the message being delivered and how to deliver the message. Organizations know that communications play an important role in the program as they focus on improving data literacy and getting people to understand their role as stewards of the data.

Delivering a data governance communications plan is a critical deliverable of many of my engagements. My clients recognize the importance of effective interactions as a critical piece of program success. Communications plans focus on orienting people to data governance, onboarding people into their governance role and ongoing communications.

The people responsible for your data governance program may be good communicators, but the people in your corporate communications group are specialists in this art. Leveraging their knowledge and ability to deliver an effective message about data governance requires that they understand the purpose and focus of your program so that they can add value and become a great data governance partner.

Project Management Office (PMO)

The Project Management Office (PMO) governs the management of projects. Sounds like a cheeseburger definition ("a burger with cheese"), but it is true. The PMO function may manage the planning process and delivery of your data governance program. This demonstrates that you are partnering with this part of the organization. This partnership typically lasts for the duration of the project activities. Once a program becomes operationalized, the PMO typically moves on to its next project to manage.

Building the action of governing data into project plans proactively assures that the project's definition, production, and use of data align with the need to execute and enforce authority over that data. The PMO is a perfect data governance partner.

Change Management Office (CMO)

If your organization has a change management department or office, they are most likely responsible for governing how the organization prepares, supports, and helps individuals, teams, and organizations to accept and embrace change. Data governance requires many organizational changes, including a shift to more formalized data, roles, processes, communications, metrics, and tools. Therefore, consider leveraging people skilled at change management as data governance partners when delivering your data governance program.

Data governance programs are only successful when the culture is adjusted or changed to recognize the value of data and formal accountability. This formalization is a significant change for many organizations. Therefore, if you have a CMO or similar department in your organization, you may consider including them in your list of data governance partners.

Key Messages

The departments mentioned in this essay can be considered data governance partners. They are not a group. Organizations that recognize partners as part of their program leverage the expertise and practices of people in the departments that are already governing something. Most often, the relationship between the program and the partner is one-on-one, but it also makes sense to engage multiple partners when necessary. Partners do not band together in a group, but they play a vital role in the success of the data governance program.

Behavior and Documentation

Some people say that data governance should be called *people governance*. The business value from data and metadata will only be appreciated when people's behavior is formalized and enforced, resulting in improved quality, confidence, and protection of the data. Data governance is all about understanding what governed data looks like, providing documentation and metadata about the data, and changing people's data habits to address the challenges they cope with every day.

The final section of this book provides important considerations for governing people's behavior and significant items to keep in mind when it comes to data governance technology and managing your metadata. The chapters in this section focus on clearly defining the characteristics of governed data, common challenges organizations face when implementing a data governance program and recording requirements and changing habits associated with managing data and data documentation.

CHAPTER 7

Governing People's Behavior

The execution and enforcement of authority over the definition, production, and usage of data (my definition of data governance) requires that the "right" people behave in the "right" way when interacting with data and metadata. The formalization of accountability (my definition of stewardship) focuses on changing people's data habits, educating them on how to achieve governed data, and helping them to address the challenges they have when working with the data.

This chapter begins with essays on the theme that the data will not govern itself and that people must change their data-related behaviors before it is too late. The remaining essays provide perspective and experience with the characteristics of well-governed data and the most common challenges that organizations face when implementing their data governance program.

Perspective: The Data Will Not Govern Itself

There is a direct relationship between the value your organization gets from its data, the trust your organization has in its data, and how formally that data is governed. This is not new news. In fact, this has always been the case. Value comes from the ability to use the data to make good decisions, predict behavior, and answer questions that improve efficiency and effectiveness. Trust comes from understanding the data, knowing the meaning of the data, where the data came from, and knowing how to use the data to improve operations.

People in the data management industry know that it takes a formal effort to ensure that the data in our analytical platforms, decision support databases, and data warehouses (among other places) are of the highest quality. They know it takes formal effort to ensure quality data in the information systems we build and the software packages we purchase and migrate our data toward. Formal effort ensures quality data is being provided through resources like master data management initiatives, improving analytical capabilities, and corralling big data resources.

Organizations know that the value of these resources will come from the data that is managed through these efforts. Yet, organizations still focus on these efforts independently and with little regard for how data can be leveraged together to improve the success of our organizations. The same data, defined and produced differently and depending on the sponsor's needs rather than the organization's strategic needs, results in siloed data resources that are difficult to integrate, share, and leverage.

This is why artificial intelligence and data-centricity are still a dream for many organizations. Organizations continue to spend large amounts of money on the technology associated with their data without formally governing their data as a valued cross-enterprise asset. Governance builds consistency. Governance builds interoperability. Governance builds value and trust in the data.

Most people recognize that the data will not govern itself.

The previous short sentences should be stated more often to substantiate the point that formal data governance requires that we focus on getting the "right" people to take the "right" actions at the "right" time with the "right" data to get the "right" outcome with the data as often as possible.

Data governance is the execution and enforcement of authority over the definition, production, and use of data and data-related assets. Execution and enforcement of authority sums it up quite well. This definition summarizes that people's actions are the focal point of data governance.

You may even consider calling the discipline "people governance" instead of data governance because it is the behavior of people associated with the definition, production, and use of the data that will improve the quality, value, and trust in the data. Formalizing people's behavior consistently leads to improvements in the value and confidence in the data. We all know that the data will not govern itself.

One way to improve the value people get, and trust people have, in the data is to improve their knowledge about the data. This includes knowledge of the data resources that are available to them and knowledge about the specific data that resides in these data resources. Metadata is the information used to improve people's knowledge of the data. Metadata exists in data catalogs, business glossaries, data dictionaries, and repositories, made up of databases, spreadsheets, and documents that describe the data.

Data documentation is an afterthought in many system development or integration efforts. Metadata is scattered across the organization, siloed from other metadata, and often not formally managed, kept up to date, or easily accessible. As a result, people do not have the metadata they need to improve efficiency and effectiveness in how they complete their job functions. Metadata is often incomplete, inconsistent, inappropriate, or unavailable. Metadata is not governed, meaning people are not formally held accountable for the data documentation or metadata. This causes problems.

The final essay in this book describes how metadata will also not govern itself.

Key Messages

Do we see a trend here? The bottom line is that data does not naturally or automatically increase in value or become more trusted without a purposeful effort. We must orchestrate the effort at the strategic and tactical levels of the organization to demonstrate value and gain people's trust at the operational level. The effort requires that people have the time, skills, and tools needed to deliver value and trust in the data. Metadata is a necessary component. In general, organizations must get their people heavily involved and invested in the need for improved data. It will not magically happen. The data will not govern itself.

Experience: Change Data Habits Before It is Too Late

The management of data is very similar to the management of one's health. One way they are similar has become very apparent to me over the years. If you do not take care of your personal well-being, poor health has a way of catching up on you. Once poor health becomes an issue, it can take a long time or even forever to get past the issues.

But what about your data? If you do not take care of your organization's data, then your organization's data health can become poor as well. If you have not been taking good care of your data's health for a long time, you may have a serious data health issue that doesn't just call for small changes to your data behavior. Poor data health might require major surgery, such as re-engineering your organization's entire data infrastructure.

Gauge Your Organization's Data Health

Just like when you go to the doctor, the first thing that must occur when gauging your organization's data health is an evaluation of your present state. This must always take place before prescribing a remedy. There are several ways to evaluate your organization's data health. Consider these three ways of evaluating your present condition:

- **Assess Best Practices**. Organizations must take a "ready, aim, fire" approach to gauging their data health, which requires defining best practices for each assessed data discipline. The steps to assess include defining why the best practice makes sense, observing and recording present practices, observing and recording opportunities for the organization to improve its data health, articulating the gap between the present practice and the best practice, and defining the risk associated with this gap. Once this assessment and analysis are complete, it is possible to use this information to determine the appropriate path to achieve best practice.

- **Use Industry Models.** You can use one of several industry models to evaluate your present data health. These models provide a basis for comparison to numerous industry-specific data management disciplines. Three industry models that I suggest for your consideration include CMMI's Data Management Maturity Model,[18] the EDM Council—DCAM,[19] and the DAMA International—Body of Knowledge (DMBOK).[20]

- **Ask Your Customers.** Ask your business and technical stakeholders what they think of how you are enabling them through each data discipline. Many organizations survey their business and technical communities regarding how they are doing and where they can be more efficient and effective. Typical surveys focus on customer satisfaction, value add, and return on investment.

Your organization's data health depends on how well you define, produce, and use your data. Improvements in data management often are related to one or more of these actions. I will use the three actions to focus on ways you can change your data habits.

Change the Way You Define Data

Good data production and good data usage depend on how well the data is defined. The likelihood that quality data will be produced decreases when the definition of the data is incomplete or written in a way that leads to data that cannot be interpreted, and thus produced by the business. The likelihood that data will be used properly also depends on quality data definitions. Quality data definitions will lead people to produce better quality data and use data the way it is defined to be used.

---

[18] http://cmmiinstitute.com/data-management-maturity.

[19] https://www.edmcouncil.org/dcam.

[20] http://dama.org/content/body-knowledge.

- **Model Your Data.** Data modeling is an important discipline that has become a fading or lost art in the field of data management. Data modeling was the healthy heart of data when I started in data management for good reason. Organizations that logically and physically model their data have well-defined data and data structures, resulting in strong definitional metadata management and efficient and effective database design. The data modeling disciple is evolving as organizations extend into new technologies and methods, including graph databases, NoSQL databases, big data sources, and the Agile project management methodology.

- **Manage Your Metadata.** Metadata management, or managing what you know about your data, is extremely beneficial to your organization's ability to understand and trust the data. It is impossible to have strong data health without focusing on managing metadata. Organizations struggle to leverage their data investments because of a lack of emphasis on building and maintaining business glossaries, data dictionaries, and data catalogs. You don't have to implement a centralized data catalog or metadata repository to provide positive benefits, but it certainly helps your data health.

- **Involvement in Agile.** The Agile project methodology can deliver high-quality projects quickly, effectively, and incrementally. Organizations typically select high-profile projects and projects that would take a long time to complete when they select this methodology, often emphasizing speed over good data health. Data lies at the heart of these projects making the attention to data quality important. Organizations evaluating their data health must look at the relationship between data management and Agile projects to find common ground that applies the appropriate amount of time and resources to focus on the data.

Change the Way You Produce Data

The era of big data calls for organizations to improve their data health and increase their ability to find and use all forms of data. These forms of data include structured and unstructured sources. Organizations are finding ways to produce new and better data from old data every time they integrate data sources to solve a problem. The rate of data growth is astonishing. This growth makes it obvious that organizations evaluating ways to change data habits should focus on data production as an area that will lead to better data health.

- **Assess Data Sources.** The ability to leverage ownership (stewardship of the data) is very important to the governance of data. Data sources that are important enough to manage and utilize for business decision-making and improving operations are also important enough to be well-documented and understood. Organizations that are changing their data habits should put time and effort into assessing existing data sources for what they know and do not know so that they can fill in the missing pieces and improve their data health.

- **Control Entry Points.** Letting bad data into systems is never a good idea. In fact, if we could stop this from happening, it would solve all our data quality problems. So where do all the data quality problems come from? The control (or lack thereof) of the entry point of data is an important contributor to the organization's data health. Whether that entry point is manual entry, data transformation, or new data sources, an organization needs to evaluate how well they manage data entry points when considering improving data quality and, thus, data health.

- **Manage Data Quality.** We can also evaluate data quality using the same three actions—definition, production, and usage. Improvement to data health can involve improving the quality of data definition, as discussed in the prior section, improving quality data production, as was just mentioned, and improving the quality of data usage through improved access, understanding, and protection. Organizations are changing their data quality habits by applying data governance to all three data actions. This is because they realize that data quality is a key contributor to data health.

Change the Way You Use Data

Some organizations focus on data usage habits first when seeking management's support for data governance. Protecting sensitive data is easy for management to understand because they recognize this action as "not optional." The same holds true for following regulatory guidelines. Management knows that the rules associated with protection and regulations are being dictated to them. However, using data for analytical purposes is a conscious decision, often made by management, that requires serious data health and discipline. Assessing your habits associated with data usage, including how well the data is understood, classified, and protected is critical to improving the value your organization gets from using its data.

- **Improve User Understanding.** Improving the organization's metadata management capabilities is one of the keys to improving the organization's understanding of the data. Organizations often begin by focusing on business glossaries and data dictionaries because they represent the understanding of a small subset of important data, such as data in their business intelligence, data warehousing, and master data environments. Therefore, this is a good place to improve understanding by focusing on metadata health associated with the most important data. Developing a rich metadata management repository requires resources similar to those needed to build a data warehouse. Evaluate what your stakeholders need to know about the data, compared to what is already recorded and made available, to improve your organization's data health.

- **Classify Your Data.** These last two aspects of changing how you use your data is tightly related. Before you can claim perfect health around protecting sensitive data, it is important to classify your data (i.e., highly classified, sensitive, public) based on rules for each classification level. Classify data first, and the rules associated with handling data per each classification must be defined, communicated to the masses, followed, and enforced to satisfy a core component of governing your organization's data.

- **Protect Sensitive Data.** Data protection is a concern of every organization. Whether the data is personally identifiable information (PII), personal health information (PHI), intellectual property (IP), or personal information that falls under the European Union's GDPR (General Data Protection Regulation), the rules associated with protecting sensitive data are forever changing, and part of your data health depends on how well you protect your data. Therefore, changing your habits associated with protecting sensitive data is a requirement of all organizations that cannot be overstated.

Key Messages

Managing your data's health is similar to managing your personal health. Most doctors will suggest that you change your habits if you are overweight and out of shape. Your health matters will not self-correct if you do not change your habits. Organizations can learn from this simple health lesson. If the organization is expected to improve its data health, it must begin by changing its habits. Organizations must change their data definition, production, and usage habits before it is too late.

Experience: Characteristics of Governing Data

Data governance means different things to different people. Sometimes organizations use the terms data governance and data stewardship interchangeably. Sometimes they use the term "non-invasive" to describe their approach to data governance. Unfortunately, there is not a single accepted standard definition for data governance.

My definition, "data governance is the execution and enforcement of authority over the management of data," is a controversial definition because of how strongly it is worded. My definition always raises the questions, "What does governed data look like?" and "What does execution and enforcement of authority really mean?"

This essay will briefly explain what it means to "govern" something. Let's start with the basic definition of "govern" from FreeDictionary.com. I wrapped the words "to" and "data" around each identifying characteristic of the definition. The identifying characteristics are the part of the definition that tells you how that term is unique or different from other terms. The wrapper around the identifying characteristics of the word "govern" makes these characteristics easier to read and it puts the characteristic into the context of data.

The following is the FreeDictionary.com definition of the word "govern" wrapped in a data context:

[to] gov·ern [data]—gov·erned, gov·ern·ing, gov·erns

Identifying characteristics:

- [To] make and administer the public policy and affairs [of data]
- [To] exercise sovereign authority [over data]
- [To] control the speed or magnitude [of data]
- [To] regulate [data]
- [To] control the actions or behavior [of data]
- [To] keep under control [data]; to restrain [data]
- [To] exercise a deciding or determining influence [on data]

- [To] exercise political authority [over data]

FreeDictionary.com [wrapper by Bob Seiner]

Let's walk through each of the eight identifying characteristics and see what it means to govern data as it relates to that specific characteristic.

1. To make and administer the public policy and affairs of data.

- **Governing data means** that data policy takes the form of written and approved corporate or organizational documents.

- **Governing data means** that you have a data governance policy. This policy may be hidden under the information security, privacy, or data classification policies.

- **Governing data means** that your organization leverages the effort invested in developing and approving the policy rather than allowing the policy to become shelfware.

2. To exercise the sovereign authority of data.

- **Governing data means** a way exists to resolve a difference of opinion on a cross-business data issue.

- **Governing data means** that somebody or some group of individuals is the authority or has the authority to make decisions concerning the data.

- **Governing data means** an escalation path exists from the operational to the tactical to the strategic levels of the organization for decision-making. Rarely does governing data require escalation of data issues to the executive level.

3. To control the speed or magnitude of data.

- **Governing data means** that data is shared according to the classification (confidential, sensitive, public) rules associated with that data.

- **Governing data means** that the creation of new versions of the same data is scrutinized closely to manage and eliminate data redundancy.

- **Governing data means** that people don't make copies of critical or confidential data that fails to follow the same scrutiny and governance as data in native form.

4. To regulate data.

- **Governing data means** that appropriate processes are put in place to regulate data and monitor the definition, production, and usage of data at all levels of an organization.

- **Governing data means** that proactive and reactive processes are defined, approved, and followed at all levels of the organization. Situations that do not follow these regulatory procedures can be identified, prevented, and resolved.

- **Governing data means** that the appropriate regulatory behaviors around data are brought to the forefront of your staff members' thought processes rather than being pushed to the back of their minds as an "inconvenience" or "nice to have."

5. To control the actions or behaviors of data.

- **Governing data means** that appropriate behaviors and actions associated with controlling data are put in place and monitored to manage the definition, production, and usage of data at all levels of the organization.

- **Governing data means** that proactive and reactive processes are defined, approved, and followed at all levels of the organization and that situations where these behaviors are not accepted and followed are identified, prevented, and resolved.

- **Governing data means** that the appropriate behaviors around data are brought to the forefront of your staff's thought processes rather than being pushed to the back of their minds as an "inconvenience" or a "nice to have."

6. To keep under control and restrain data.

- **Governing data means** that access to data is managed, secured, and auditable by classification and that processes and responsibilities are put in place to ensure access privileges are granted only to appropriate individuals.

- **Governing data means** that all individuals understand the rules associated with importing data into spreadsheets, loading data to laptops, transmitting data, or any other activity that removes data from the native source.

- **Governing data means** that the rules associated with controlling hard-copy versions of data are well documented and communicated to individuals who generate, receive, or distribute these hard copies.

7. To exercise a deciding or determining influence of data.

- **Governing data means** that the right people are involved at the right time for the right reasons to ensure that the right decisions are made about the right data.

- **Governing data means** that the information about who does what with the data is completely recorded, shared, and understood across the organization.

- **Governing data means** that a formal escalation path exists for known data issues that move from operational to tactical to strategic and to the persons identified as the authorities on that specific use of the data.

8. To exercise political authority over data.

- **Governing data means** that somebody or some group of people have the authority to make decisions about data that impacts the enterprise.

- **Governing data means** that the political nature of decision-making is leveraged in making tactical and strategic decisions that best benefit the enterprise.

- **Governing data means** a formal escalation path exists for known data issues that move from operational (business unit specific) to tactical (cross-business unit) to strategic (enterprise) and to persons identified as the authorities on that specific use of that data.

Key Messages

This essay briefly explains what it means to "govern" something. The definition of the word lays out several characteristics that support my definition shared throughout this book. To execute and enforce authority over data, the organization must follow many of the identifying characteristics of what it means to govern something.

The next time somebody asks you to tell them the difference between governed and ungoverned data, do not be afraid to pull out the list in this essay and make a case for why the organization's data must follow the dictionary definition of the word "govern."

Experience: Common Data Governance Challenges

Organizations delivering formal data governance programs often experience many challenges. The challenges differ from organization to organization. However, several challenges appear often. This essay quickly spells out those common data governance challenges.

Before I begin, it makes sense to recognize that every data environment is different. Organizations have different levels of maturity associated with each challenge. For that reason, I have provided a simple chart below and suggest that you evaluate the status of your organizations associated with each challenge. A darker color means you are at risk of the challenge defeating your chance of success. A mid-darkness color means that the way you are addressing the challenge needs work, and lighter color means that you are addressing the challenge in an acceptable way. You can also use the colors red, yellow, and green, or a numbering system to indicate your level of maturity.

The challenges presented in the list below and in Figure 4-1 are a good starting point for delivering practical and pragmatic best practices for forming a formal data governance program.

Common challenges of implementing a formal data governance program include:

- Lack of Data Leadership
- Understanding Business Value of Data Governance
- Defining the Purpose of Data Governance and the Pain Caused by Data
- Senior Management Support, Sponsorship, and Understanding
- Budgets and Ownership
- People Think IT Owns the Data
- Lack of Data Documentation
- Resources to Apply to Data Governance

Common Data Governance Challenges

Lack of Data Leadership	Budgets and Ownership
Understanding Business Value of Data Governance	People Think IT Owns the Data
Recognizing the Need / Pain Caused By Data	Lack of Data Documentation
Senior Management Support, Sponsorship, Understanding	Resources to Apply to Data Governance

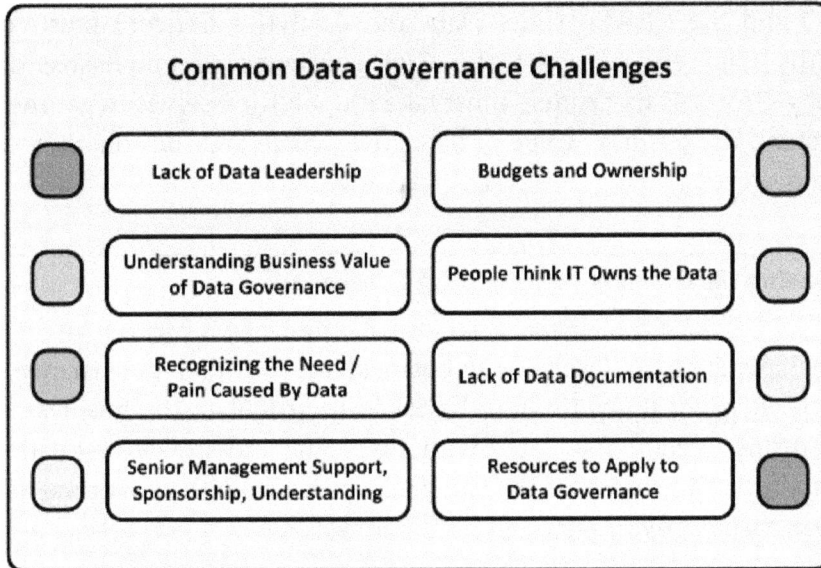

Figure 4-1. Common Data Governance Challenges

Let's go through each of these common data governance challenges.

Lack of Data Leadership

Data leadership is a challenge facing many organizations. Organizations are slowly embracing the idea that they need people to be responsible for their data and analytics beyond the technology required to leverage and protect data. That is why the Chief Data Officer (CDO) role is slowly working its way up to the level of prominence generally and historically reserved for the Chief Information Officer (CIO).

My friend, data leadership thought-leader, Anthony Algmin, summarized the challenge of the lack of data leadership this way: "The challenge of Data Leadership goes beyond working with data appropriately. We must orchestrate the many data activities to maximize the impact to the business."

In organizations where 'the business' and IT are constantly at odds with one another, this is no simple feat.

The CDO and the CDAO (Chief Data and Analytics Officer) must focus on leading the data efforts while the CIO continues to emphasize directing technology efforts. Data Leaders must take it upon themselves to get their peers to understand the business value of data governance and the role they will play in program success.

Understanding the Business Value of Data Governance

Another challenge is to describe the business value of data governance quickly and simply. It is not uncommon to be asked to articulate the business value in financial terms directly associated with governing and stewarding data. This is not an easy task. Consider that the value may come from the governed data itself rather than the act governing it.

Organizations must look at the expected value from other data-focused investments. The larger investment is often in digital and business transformations, upgraded ERP systems, artificial intelligence and machine learning, business intelligence and master data, analytics and data science. Organizations often do not achieve the expected level of return from these investments if the data is ungoverned.

Investments that only focus on technology will not improve the quality and value of your present data. They will, however, highlight data deficiencies. As I have stated in prior essays, the data will not govern itself. This should be enough, but management seems to want more.

Therefore, we attempt to give them more. We attempt to quantify the data in several ways including measuring the organization's confidence in data, the quality and consistency of the data, people's ability to operate efficiently and effectively with the data, how long it takes to gain access to data, the level of understanding of the data that in available to them, how the data is classified, and how it must be handled—to share a few of those ways. We find other ways to demonstrate the business value of data governance when looking at the ROI of other investments.

Defining the Purpose of Data Governance

One challenge that is easy to address is to define the purpose of data governance at your organization. You must be able to quickly answer the question, "Why are we building a data governance program?" The answer results in a data governance purpose statement. Here are a few samples of short purpose statements:

The purpose of our data governance program is to:

- Use strategic data with confidence.
- Protect classified information.
- Improve the delivery of high quality, usable data.
- Ensure the data is trusted and accessible by the appropriate people.

Define the Pain Caused by Data

Another challenge is to understand the pain caused by data. Ask people about their challenges in their jobs and with data. Earlier in the book, I mentioned questions to ask, including "What can't you do?" and "What would you do?" if people had efficient and effective access to data they trusted. Questions like these often produce open conversations that result in 1) learning about the pains people feel associated with how they work with data and 2) providing insight into how data governance will achieve its purpose.

The purpose of data governance must focus on a business need and address the pain people are feeling. The only way to learn the data pain of the business is to ask them.

Senior Management Support, Sponsorship, and Understanding

I have included essays in both books directed at addressing this challenge. Getting senior management to support, sponsor, and understand what it will take to apply formal governance to critical data is a constant challenge at many organizations. Support and sponsorship often come early while getting senior management to understand what a governed and stewarded data landscape looks like and what it will take to get there requires planning and education.

Every organization should consider this as best practice when standing up their data governance program. Your data governance program will be at risk if you do not achieve a high-level of senior management support, sponsorship, and understanding of data governance and the actions of your program.

Budgets and Ownership

Many organizations face the challenge of who will pay for data governance. One question I get often is where data governance should live in the organization. The normal answers are "IT" and "the business." Some people believe that your governance program will fail if it is budgeted (and therefore lands) under Information Technology (IT). I am not one of those people.

The answer of "the business" is very vague but also the answer that is given most often. Data governance programs often reside in Finance, Risk Management, Operations, Enterprise Analytics, or other business areas. The ownership of data governance must reside somewhere, meaning that the program's administration must be somebody's formal responsibility.

Data governance has to be owned and paid for by somebody. If that somebody is IT, you must break the perception that IT "owns the data." IT may "own" the administration of data governance, but there should be recognition that the business must steward and be accountable for the data. This is a point I made in the first book when I wrote about how "everybody is a data steward." People who define, produce, and use the data are stewards if they are held formally accountable for how they define, produce, and use it. These are mostly business people.

People Think IT Owns the Data

This challenge is related to the previous challenge. There is a common belief in many organizations that IT owns the data and that business people are just users of the data. I want to make it clear that from my experience this premise is false. Although this has been the perception over the years, we as practitioners should make it our mission to dispel this myth.

IT has a lot of responsibility for the data, but defining, producing, and using the business data are not typically included in those responsibilities. IT is responsible for providing the technology required to address the definition, production, and use of business data. But almost all practitioners agree that business people should be responsible for working alongside IT to define data and data requirements, produce high-quality data, and use data for operational and decision-making purposes.

Lack of Data Documentation

Data documentation is certainly a challenge. I often refer to data documentation as metadata because data about the data must be recorded somewhere for it to become beneficial to the stewards of the data. There are many categories of metadata that can originate inside and outside tools in your environment. Selecting the appropriate categories that will result in business value and determining how much metadata to record and make available is an early challenge.

Governing the metadata is a challenge for many organizations as well. Someone must be formally responsible for defining what metadata must be collected. Someone must be formally accountable for producing that metadata, and somebody must be formally accountable for using the metadata. Data documentation is a challenge every organization must address.

Resources to Apply to Data Governance

I have stated several times in this book that data and metadata will not govern itself. Somebody must be held formally accountable if your organization expects sustainable success in governing these assets. Organizations that allocate dedicated resources do better and move faster than those that find someone to take the responsibility beyond their other job functions and only allow a small percentage of their time to the program.

Beyond the administrator, there will likely need to be strategic and tactical level representation in the program and time allocated to engage the data stewards that define, produce, and use data as part of their jobs. An effective data governance administrator addresses this challenge and knows who these stewards are and how and when to engage them. You can read about a complete set of roles and responsibilities in the essay data governance roles and responsibilities.

Key Messages

Organizations implementing data governance programs face many challenges as they get started and as their program mature. This essay addresses several common data governance challenges and provides a simple graphic to use to highlight the status of where the organization compares to the acknowledged challenge.

Perspective: Progressive Principles for Protecting Data

There are many reasons why organizations deliver formal data governance programs. Typical reasons include: to improve the quality of data, to improve analytical capabilities, to resolve known issues, to enforce accountability for data, to ensure regulatory compliance, and more. Data protection has been steadily rising to the surface as a most important and an easier place to start a formal program. I didn't say "easy." I said, "easier." Let me explain.

First of all, gaining consensus on the need to protect data is an easy decision. The government is telling you that you must protect sensitive data and be able to prove you are doing so. There are lots of rules around protecting data. Everybody needs to be aware that there are rules, be told the rules, be told how to follow the rules and follow the rules. Sounds pretty easy.

That is, unless your organization has never formally protected sensitive data before.

The following principles are progressive statements associated with governance and behavioral aspects of protecting data. You will quickly notice that these statements build on each other and can become the basis for protecting data through formal data governance.

The principles are:

- **Your customers think that you are protecting their data.** You will lose your customers if they have the slightest notion that their data is not safe while under your care. I have always said that auditors are your friends. I say this because auditors are people in your organization who can tell you if you are protecting your data in a reportable and compliant way.

- I suggest engaging your internal auditors proactively rather than waiting for an assessment report from an external source (read—bad news!). The chances are that you and your organization already know if you are doing a "good enough" job of protecting your customer's personal information. It is not enough these days for customers to trust that you are protecting their data.

- **The government says you must protect their data.** A quick Google search on "protect customer data" returns millions of results, mostly from companies looking to help you protect your data. Most countries have adopted comprehensive data protection laws, including nearly every country in Europe and Latin America. The U.S. is noteworthy for not adopting a comprehensive privacy law. Instead, the U.S. has adopted laws specifically targeted at financial, medical, political, and internet privacy.

- Specific privacy is even guaranteed in the Constitution of the United States. The government takes privacy very seriously, and the rules are getting stricter. I am guessing that the day is coming, if it is not already here, that the government will require that all organizations demonstrate that they are following the law and protecting their customer data.

- **Senior leadership says we will protect their data.** This principle may not be based on fact. It is my experience that senior leadership *must say* that their organization protects sensitive customer data, but they may be less certain that their data is being protected appropriately. Ensuring that their organization is protecting data requires that everyone in the organization is aware of the rules and held formally accountable for how they handle sensitive data.

- In many organizations, people are mostly unaware of the specifics of the rules unless there are governance activities targeted at making them aware of the rules and changing their behavior. Sensitive data can includes personally identifiable information (PII), personal health information (PHI), and increasingly intellectual property (IP), to name just a few types. Whatever industry you are in, it is likely that some data must be protected.

- **Data governance tells us how to protect data.** While it is common knowledge that data governance can do many things to improve the value of your organization's data, organizations are still looking for ways to get started in governing their data. Protecting sensitive data is a great way to get started. If you agree that peoples' behaviors must change for data to be protected, then the organization must focus on specific activities that assure that type of change. The activities include defining roles and responsibilities, best practices, communications, and an awareness plan specifically around data governance (and data protection), developing thorough education, and delivering these materials.

- Data governance, defined by me as the "formal execution and enforcement of authority over the management of data," should include a protection component. Data governance tells us how to protect data. Protecting data starts with increasing people's awareness of the data protection rules and how to enforce those rules.

Key Messages

In this essay, I shared four progressive principles that assure the connection between data governance and the protection of data. Most organizations have programs focusing on information security, privacy, compliance, and risk management. Partners of your data governance program are providing these governing activities.

Remember that your customers think you are protecting their data, the government says that you must protect their data, and your management already says that you are protecting their data. The next step is to use your data governance to solidify how you protect their data.

Chapter 8

Technology and Metadata (Data Documentation)

Technology and metadata are enablers for data governance program success. Data technologies such as data catalogs, metadata repositories, and data mesh and fabric are valuable instruments that advance the effective definition, production, and use of enterprise data as an appreciated asset. Technology and metadata appear in the Non-Invasive Data Governance Framework tools column shared in Chapter 1.

The book's final chapter focuses on several important considerations regarding the effective use of technology and metadata to enhance your data governance program. The essays in this chapter address the data governance challenges associated with large language models (LLMs), the governance of data mesh and data fabric, the questions to answer when governed and trusted metadata is made available to the data stewards of the organization, and considerations for metadata tool requirements. The final essay reminds you that, just like the data, the metadata will not govern itself.

Perspective: Data Governance Challenges
Associated with Large Language Models (LLMs)

This essay has been labeled as a perspective essay because, at the time of the publishing of this book, a limited number of organizations have aligned the attention of their data governance programs with Large Language Models (LLMs). Significant content focuses on the development, deployment, and use of LLMs. There is also content written about the ethical, privacy, bias, and power concerns people have with the use of LLMs. This essay focuses on the relationship between the discipline of data governance and the use of LLMs.

As I have mentioned earlier in this book, data governance is the execution and enforcement of authority over the definition, production, and usage of data. Data governance involves holding people formally accountable for the actions they take with data through stewardship and requires a determined effort to manage the information you have about your data. Data governance is gradually becoming an important consideration associated with the benefits of LLMs.

Large language models are artificial intelligence systems trained on massive amounts of data and capable of generating human-like interaction through text. LLMs use machine learning (ML) algorithms to analyze patterns in data and learn how to generate text similar to what a human might write or say. Using LLMs can create significant data governance challenges, particularly regarding data quality, data privacy, and ethical considerations.

Some of the better-known LLMs include GPT-3 (Generative Pre-trained Transformer 3), ChatGPT (same acronym applies), and BERT (Bidirectional Encoder Representations from Transformers), which have been used, with varying levels of skepticism, for a variety of applications, such as language translation, content generation, and chatbots. In this essay, I will address the relationship between data governance and LLMs and discuss some of the key considerations for organizations seeking to implement LLM technologies.

In the past, when I have written about my experiences implementing data governance programs, I typically focus on how the programs govern organizational data assets to ensure they are accurate, consistent, secure, and compliant with legal and regulatory requirements. I have written about data governance policies, procedures, best practices, tools, and technologies used to support these activities. Data governance is critical for ensuring that data is available when needed, is of sufficient quality to support decision-making, and is protected from unauthorized access or misuse. These same topics are relevant when LLMs enter the conversation.

LLMs are formidable tools that use complicated algorithms to identify patterns and relationships in data and language. LLMs have shown remarkable success in generating human-like text, leading to their adoption in a wide range of industries. Applying data governance to the use of LLMs presents organizations with new challenges.

These challenges include:

- Data Stewardship Challenges
- Data Documentation Challenges
- Data Risk, Privacy, and Security Challenges
- Data Quality Challenges
- Third-Party and Vendor Challenges
- Operational Efficiency Challenges

Since many organizations have not yet addressed the data governance challenges associated with LLMs, and to demonstrate the effectiveness of the technology, an LLM provided input into the details of the following challenges. Limited references to non-invasive data governance have been inserted, highlighting the point that the data challenges presented by LLMs are consistent across all approaches to data governance.

Data Stewardship Challenges

LLMs are built on large volumes of data, increasing the need for active data stewardship practices focused on ensuring that the data is governed ethically and responsibly across that volume. Stewardship refers to the formalization of accountability for the practice of defining, producing, and using data throughout its lifecycle, and is critical to ensuring that LLMs are used responsibly and effectively.

Data stewardship challenges include:

- **Data quality and accuracy**: LLMs rely on large amounts of data to generate accurate and meaningful insights. Ensuring the quality and accuracy of this data is essential to the effectiveness of the model. However, data quality issues can arise at various stages of the data lifecycle, including data collection, processing, and labeling. Organizations must hold people formally accountable to address the robust data quality assurance processes to mitigate these risks.

- **Data bias and fairness**: LLMs can be trained on biased or unrepresentative datasets, resulting in biased or unfair outputs. These biases can perpetuate existing inequalities and discrimination and harm the organization's reputation. Stewards must implement appropriate data labeling and selection processes, as well as ongoing monitoring and auditing, to ensure that the model is fair and unbiased.

- **Data privacy and security**: LLMs often require access to sensitive data, such as personal information or confidential business data. Ensuring the privacy and security of this data is essential to maintain trust with customers and stakeholders. Stewards must be accountable for implementing appropriate data privacy and security policies, such as data encryption, access controls, and data anonymization.

- **Data ownership and licensing**: LLMs may incorporate data from third-party sources or use open-source datasets. Ensuring the organization has the appropriate ownership and licensing rights for this data is essential to avoid legal or reputational risks. Through the stewarding of LLM as a data resource, organizations must implement appropriate data licensing and usage agreements and ensure that the necessary permissions and consents are obtained.

- **Data governance and oversight**: LLMs require ongoing governance and oversight to ensure they are used effectively and responsibly. This may include establishing clear roles and responsibilities for data stewardship, implementing appropriate monitoring and reporting processes, and ensuring that the model is aligned with organizational values and ethics.

Data Documentation Challenges

LLMs rely heavily on large amounts of data, and their efficacy and precision depend on the quality and completeness of the data they rely on. Data documentation is critical to the development, deployment, and ongoing use of LLMs.

Data documentation challenges include:

- **Complex data processing pipelines**: LLMs require complex data processing pipelines, which make it challenging to document the data effectively. These pipelines involve multiple data sources, processing steps, and model training processes, making it difficult to track the origin of the data and understand how it was transformed.

- **Large and diverse datasets**: LLMs rely on large and diverse datasets to generate accurate and meaningful insights. Managing and documenting these datasets can be challenging, particularly if they are sourced from multiple locations or involve sensitive data. Organizations must implement appropriate data documentation practices to ensure the datasets are well-documented, accessible, and traceable.

- **Rapidly evolving models**: LLMs constantly evolve as new data is added and new models are developed. This presents the challenges of keeping data documentation up to date to ensure that it accurately reflects the current model. Keeping up with these changes can be challenging, particularly if the model is used by multiple teams or across several departments.

- **Data governance and oversight**: LLMs require ongoing governance and oversight to ensure they are used effectively and responsibly. This includes documenting data usage policies, model performance metrics, and any relevant ethical considerations. Ensuring that this documentation is comprehensive and up to date can be challenging, particularly if the model is used across multiple teams or departments.

Data Risk, Privacy, and Security Challenges

LLMs may hold critical information about an organization's customers, members, and associates, product and material data, intellectual property, and financial and personal information, making them an attractive target for cyber-attacks. If the LLM is not properly secured, intruders can steal sensitive data or inject malware into the system, potentially leading to financial loss, regulatory fines, or reputational damage.

Data risk, privacy, and security challenges include:

- **Data privacy**: LLMs require large volumes of text data, including personally identifiable information (PII) such as names, addresses, and other personal data. If this data is not properly secured, it can be at risk of being accessed or stolen by unauthorized parties.

- **Malicious content generation**: LLMs can be used to generate malicious content, such as spam emails, phishing messages, or fake news articles. This can be particularly concerning when the content generated by LLMs is used to manipulate public opinion or influence important decision-making processes.

- **Adversarial attacks**: LLMs are vulnerable to adversarial attacks, which involve intentionally modifying the input data to trick the model into producing incorrect or malicious output. For example, an adversarial attack could be used to modify text data in a way that causes the LLM to generate offensive or misleading content.

- **Model theft**: LLMs are valuable intellectual property, and the models themselves can be at risk of being stolen or reverse-engineered. If an unauthorized party gains access to an LLM, they could potentially use it to generate content without proper authorization or oversight.

- **Ethical concerns**: LLMs can generate text data that is difficult to distinguish from text written by humans. This raises ethical concerns around the use of LLMs for deception or other unethical purposes, such as generating fake reviews or social media posts.

Data Quality Challenges

LLMs are susceptible to data quality issues, such as inaccurate, incomplete, or inconsistent data. This can occur due to entry errors, data duplication, or data formatting issues, leading to incorrect or unreliable results when using the LLM for reporting, analytics, or decision-making.

Data quality challenges include:

- **Bias**: LLMs learn biases and stereotypes from the data they are fed, which can affect the content they generate. An LLM trained on text that includes biased language or topics may generate biased or stereotyped content.

- **Incomplete or inaccurate data**: LLMs require large volumes of high-quality data to learn from. If the data used to train the LLM is incomplete or inaccurate, it can lead to poor performance or errors in the generated text. LLMs trained on text data that includes errors or omissions may generate text that contains factual inaccuracies or logical inconsistencies.

- **Domain-specificity**: LLMs are typically trained on large datasets that cover a broad range of topics and domains. However, if the LLM is used in a specific domain or context, it may not have access to the relevant data needed to generate accurate or relevant text. An LLM trained on general text data may not be able to generate accurate legal or medical language without further training on specialized datasets.

- **Noise**: Large datasets can contain irrelevant or extraneous data, which can affect the performance of LLMs. Noise can also come in the form of misspellings, typos, or formatting errors in the data, leading to errors in the generated text.

- **Lack of diversity**: LLMs trained on a narrow range of data can limit their ability to generate diverse and nuanced content. LLMs trained only on text written by a particular group of authors may not be able to generate text in other styles or voices.

Third-Party and Vendor Challenges

Organizations often rely on third-party vendors to provide and manage their LLMs, which can introduce additional challenges. If the vendor experiences a data breach or other security incident, it can compromise the organization's data and put them at risk.

Third-party and vendor challenges include:

- **Data security and privacy**: When organizations share their data with third-party vendors to develop or use LLMs, they can expose themselves to data security and privacy risks. Vendors may not have the same level of security measures or privacy protocols in place, which could result in data breaches or other security incidents.

- **Data ownership and licensing**: Ownership and licensing of data used in LLMs can be complex, particularly when multiple parties are involved. Organizations must ensure that they have appropriate ownership and licensing agreements in place with their vendors and a clear understanding of how their data will be used and who owns the resulting LLMs.

- **Quality control and performance**: Organizations must ensure that their vendors develop and use LLMs that meet their quality and performance standards. This can require implementing quality control measures and monitoring vendor performance to ensure that LLMs deliver the expected results.

- **Compliance and regulatory risks**: Depending on the application or industry, organizations can be subject to specific regulations or standards that impact their use of LLMs. Organizations may face legal or regulatory risks if their vendors are not compliant with these regulations or standards.

- **Intellectual property rights**: Ownership and licensing of LLMs can present challenges, particularly when multiple parties are involved. Organizations must ensure that they have appropriate ownership and licensing agreements with their vendors and do not infringe on the intellectual property rights of others.

Operational Inefficiency Challenges

LLMs can become unwieldy and difficult to manage over time, particularly if they are not regularly maintained and updated. This can lead to operational inefficiencies, such as slow response times, increased costs, or difficulty extracting useful insights from the data.

- **High computational requirements**: LLMs require significant computational resources, including high-performance computing infrastructure, specialized hardware, and storage. These requirements can be costly, both in terms of infrastructure investments and ongoing operational expenses.

- **Complex data processing**: LLMs rely on large amounts of data, which must be processed and formatted in a specific way to be usable by the model. This data processing can be time-consuming and require specialized expertise, resulting in operational inefficiencies.

- **Model training and optimization**: LLMs must be trained on large datasets, which can take weeks or months to complete. This training process requires significant computational resources, as well as specialized expertise in machine learning and natural language processing.

- **Maintenance and updates**: LLMs require ongoing maintenance and updates to ensure they continue performing effectively. This may include monitoring performance, identifying and addressing errors or biases, and updating the model to reflect underlying data or business needs changes.

- **Integration with existing systems**: LLMs must be integrated with existing systems and workflows to be effective. This integration can be complex and require significant coordination between different teams or departments, resulting in operational inefficiencies.

Key Messages

To effectively manage the data governance challenges associated with LLMs, organizations must consider establishing a strong data governance program presence that addresses the challenges presented in this essay: data stewardship, data documentation, data risk, privacy, and security, data quality, third-party and vendor, and operational efficiency. Large language models (LLMs) are here to stay. As organizations begin to embrace their use and integrate them into operations, data governance programs must be proactive and consider how they will address many of the challenges presented by using this technology.

Experience: Governing Data Mesh and Fabric

The terms "Data Mesh" and "Data Fabric" are the most recent names describing techniques to help organizations manage their data. In this essay I focus on the overlap and relationship between data governance, data fabric, and data mesh, and the role of data as the soul of this business transformation.

The term "governance" focuses attention on people's behavior. Governance is often connected with power and control. While data fabric is technology-centric and data mesh focuses on organizational change, it makes sense to address organizational change first as mesh concentrates on getting people to alter their present behavior. After describing the association between governance and mesh, we will be better prepared to address the association between governance and fabric. This order is consistent with how organizations should apply governance to these two distinct but complementary techniques.

Data Governance and Data Mesh

Many organizations separate their operational data from their analytical data. Data for reporting purposes has always been separated logically and physically from data used to support organizational operations. From the past days of the data warehouse to the present days of data science and analytical platforms, data used to make decisions has been architected differently than data designed to support business functions and processes.

Data mesh architecture originated from the concept of placing the responsibility for the data with the people in the closest proximity to the data. The terms "decentralization" and "distribution of accountability" lie at the heart of mesh architecture. This premise is directly connected to data stewardship, a core tenet of data governance. Organizations that formalize accountability for data definition, production, and use as a driving factor in governing their data are ahead of organizations that avoid stewardship as the basis for their data governance programs.

Organizations looking to improve overall efficiency and effectiveness often operate in a decentralized fashion. Organizations narrow the impact of continuous change by decomposing the business into business domains. Domains of data are tactical considerations for data governance, while stewarding those data domains as cross-organizational assets become the most difficult aspect of governing data. Ownership of data by a business function may improve effectiveness but can lead to silos of data that cannot be used to view the organization as a whole.

That is where data governance must be applied to data mesh. Effective governance requires that the activities of business domain data owners be coordinated across the organization. This coordination does not happen naturally and requires a purposeful effort to drive cooperation. Formalized accountability for data (stewardship) within a business data domain and across business domains is required to achieve the level of formal data-related behavior (governance) necessary to implement a fully controlled data landscape.

Data Governance and Data Fabric

A data fabric is a set of services and architecture that deliver reliable capabilities across data environments. The architectural aspects of data fabric require standardization of data practices across data storage platforms and devices used to access that data. Standardization as a service requires the execution and enforcement of authority. In other words, governance over the data. Data fabric being technical by definition, does not eliminate the need for formalized accountability for the services and the architecture.

Data fabrics are deployed to optimize access to data distributed across platforms and logically deliver an orchestrated view of the data to enable self-service by stakeholders. Fabrics empower data scientists to access data with improved efficiency and effectiveness and eliminate many complexities resulting from attempting to access data silos. Similar to data mesh, implementing these capabilities requires the coordination and cooperation of formal data stewards and a governed data ecosystem.

Since data fabric architecture aims to democratize and fully exploit and leverage the most important data resources, reducing complexity requires consistency and standardization enforced through authority and formalized accountability for data management practices. These practices improve data quality, understanding and insights, control and access, classification, protection, and security. Implementing an effective data fabric mimics the goals of effective data governance.

Data fabric is a relatively new model that streamlines and incorporates next-gen enterprise data management (EDM) and delivers data across an assembly of endpoints, including both on-prem and cloud-based environments. Data fabric is an architecture and a set of services that relieves physical limitations, provides uniform access to data, and accelerates digital transformation.[21]

Key Messages

This essay covers the overlap and relationship between data governance, data fabric, and data mesh, and the role of data as the soul of business transformation. The availability of people and other resources to focus on building out successful data mesh and data fabric is a requirement for success. The guidance toward governed coordination and cooperation of these people is imperative to moving the organization forward to leverage its data to its fullest extent.

---

[21] Paraphrased from the overview of E-Book, Tittel, Ed. Data Fabric for Dummies (Hitachi Vantara Special Edition).

Experience: Questions Metadata Can Answer

The world of information technology has "grown up" dramatically in the last twenty-five years. From the days of punch cards and deck readers (I am old!), to the world of digital business, data and corporate intelligence, big data, artificial intelligence, machine learning, data mesh, and fabric—one might believe they have seen it all.

But not even close. One can only imagine what the next twenty-five years have in store for us. The need to manage data, information, and knowledge will be a solid business driver for the foreseeable future. An organization's ability to manage its data, information, and knowledge will determine its success.

Organizations need to know what data they have to manage their data, information, and knowledge. Organizations need to know precisely how their data is being used and how that data can be leveraged to create a competitive advantage. Much of this knowledge exists in the form of metadata. Metadata, to some, is "data about the data." Or, as I define metadata, "data stored in IT tools that improve both the business and technical understanding of data and data-related assets."

When managed effectively, metadata answers many of the questions people have about your organization's data and metadata becomes the key to increasing the confidence and trust people have in the data they use. Planning for how your organization will manage and govern metadata improves the likelihood that your data governance and metadata management programs will deliver value to data stakeholders across your organization.

A metadata plan must include identifying the questions people will ask about the data and questions that metadata will answer. This essay addresses several categories of metadata that should receive attention at the beginning of your metadata journey, the questions people will ask about your data, and the questions metadata can answer.

Metadata Categories

I have separated the questions into six categories. If these categories do not suit your needs, organize your questions in a way that makes sense to your organization. For example, metadata about the movement of data is included in my definition category because knowing where the data came from and how it has been manipulated before it reaches the location where you access the data logically falls under the definition category.

The six categories I selected include:

- Business Data Definition Metadata
- Data Structure Metadata
- Data Governance and Stewardship Metadata
- Reporting and Analysis Metadata
- Business Rules Metadata
- Rationalization Metadata

Before Reading the Questions

The categories of questions are important. However, there are a few related questions that you may want to consider asking for each of the questions in the categories. The answers to these questions may provide you with the information you need to make the business case for managing your metadata.

While you are reading through the categories, ask yourself three simple questions:

- Can my organization answer these questions?
- What does it cost for my organization to answer these questions?
- What is the result when we cannot answer these questions?

You will be surprised at how simple it becomes to justify metadata management if you can look at your answers to these three questions in relation to the questions provided below. Many of the questions I will share could fall under multiple categories. And there will be other questions I have not listed here that can be included under the categories. Consider starting your own list of questions metadata can answer and ask yourself the three questions above to justify the effort that will go into managing your metadata.

Business Data Definition Metadata

Business data definition metadata describes the logical and physical characteristics of the data, as well as the path the data has taken to reach its target. The logical characteristics focus on data taxonomies, business glossaries of terminology, data dictionaries for business data resources, repositories of data standards and business rules, and the connection between logical and physical data structures. The physical characteristics of the data are detailed in the data structure category. The movement metadata focuses on source-to-target mapping and the actions that have been taken on the data on its way to the target.

This is the first category of metadata questions that many organizations request and deliver as it improves data discoverability, utility, and trust in their data. Business users often ask these types of questions about business data definition:

- What data does my organization have?
- How is the data of the organization organized?
- How is data related to other data?
- What is the business definition of the data?
- What data is considered critical?
- What are the physical attributes of the data?
- What business rules are associated with the data?
- What is the data quality standard for the data?
- What is the quality of the data?
- Do the data elements have restrictive domains?
- What are the allowable values for the data?

- Where did my data originate? What system or database did it come from?
- How was the data manipulated (transformed) on its journey to the target?
- Who was allowed to change this data and when did it change?
- What field(s) was used to populate this data, or was the field derived?
- How was the data derived? Using calculation, conditionals, or both?
- Is the value of this data dependent on the values of other data? What data and how?

Data Structure Metadata

Data structure metadata describes the physical data. Data structure metadata is stored inside a technology data platform or within a product's database catalog. Developers and database administrators access and maintain this metadata using database management toolsets. Business users access this metadata, including people that build queries or use analytics tools to examine and report from the data.

Business users often ask these types of questions about physical data structures:

- What databases exist?
- Where is the data stored?
- What are the names of the tables in the database?
- What columns are on the tables?
- What are the table keys and what other indexes exist?
- How is this data related to other data?
- What views exist?
- When was the database structure last updated?
- What is the history of changes to the data structure?

Data Governance and Stewardship Metadata

Governance and stewardship metadata describe the relationships between people and data in terms of subject matter expertise, data authority, data ownership, and data stewardship. Data about the relationships between people and data is metadata that answers the most basic and often asked question, "Who owns the data?" Organizations record metadata about "who does what" with their data to demonstrate who is governing the data and how the data is being governed.

Data stewardship metadata describes the people in the organization who are accountable for defining, producing, and using the data. Organizations seldom maintain data stewardship metadata, and those managing this type often use desktop databases and spreadsheets. Data catalogs are becoming the tool of choice to store data stewardship metadata.

- Who do you contact if you have a question about the data?
- Who is responsible for the definition of the data?
- Who is accountable for the data production?
- Who uses the data and who do they share the data with?
- Who has the authority to make decisions about the data?
- Who is responsible for mapping data across systems and assigning values for the data?

Reporting and Analysis Metadata

This category of metadata provides an inventory of the organization's reporting and analysis artifacts and capabilities. This type of metadata describes the reports being created, the dashboards being shared, the analysis being conducted, and where to locate metadata intended to improve the organization's ability to utilize its reporting and analytical capabilities.

This category of metadata also describes the steps to gain access to the reports and analysis, the description of how the data can be interpreted, available tools, descriptions of reports, etc. Reporting and analysis metadata typically is found within reporting tools and in traditional types of documentation (i.e., desktop databases, word processing, and spreadsheets).

- What reports are being produced or analysis is being completed?
- What is the description and purpose of a report or analysis?
- How do I access the reports or analysis?
- What steps should be taken to get authorization to use the data?
- How do the reports and analysis select, organize/sort, group, total and display the data?
- What data was used by a specific report or set of analyses?
- When was the report or analysis last updated?
- Do I have to execute the report or analysis myself or are the resulting artifacts already available?

Business Rules Metadata

Business rule metadata describes how the business operates and the constraints that apply to an organization. Business rules describe data relationships and domain guidelines that define the business use of data. Business rule metadata typically exists in a modeling tool or business rules engines, often in unstructured documents and spreadsheets.

- What is the relationship between business activities and sets of data?
- What is the cardinality of that relationship (1:1, 1:M, M:M)?
- What are the business conditions under which a piece of data can take on certain values?
- What values can a piece of data take on? What are the meanings of the values?
- How is data created, updated, and deleted?
- When are rules established? Who establishes the rules?

Rationalization Metadata

My definition of rationalization is "to make sense of something." Organizations need to make sense of their data. Rationalization metadata describes how data is common and related to other data across the enterprise. Similar data often exists in multiple systems, with multiple definitions, and in multiple formats. Making sense of data requires that the similarities and differences are well documented and available to people making decisions from the data.

For example, a typical question of "How many widgets did we sell?" can be answered in different ways depending on your definition and the business context of a "widget" and a "sale." The answer to this question depends on the data source that was used and how these concepts are defined and recorded in the data. Rationalization metadata can describe the degree to which the data is the same and different across the organization.

Rationalization metadata simply focuses on making connections between metadata stored in your metadata tool. The connections between the metadata can be assisted and recorded through automation, or the actions of rationalizing data and metadata may be manual. Rationalization metadata is often stored in business glossaries, data dictionaries, other metadata repositories, and traditional types of documentation.

- How does the data I am using compare to similarly defined data across the organization?
- Why are we getting different results for the same question asked of multiple people?
- What other data exists that may be related to the data I am using?
- What are the standards for the data definition, production, and usage I am using?
- How does the data I am using compare to the definition, production, and usage standards?
- How can I navigate through the metadata to find the data that I need?

Key Messages

When planning your metadata management journey, it makes sense to begin by identifying the questions people will ask about your organization's data. This essay addressed several categories of metadata that should receive attention at the beginning of your journey, the questions people will ask about your data, and the questions metadata can answer.

Metadata answers many of the questions people have about your organization's data and is the key to increasing the confidence and trust people have in the data they use. Planning for how your organization will manage and govern metadata through a thorough understanding of the questions metadata answer improves the likelihood that your metadata management programs will deliver value to data stakeholders across your organization.

Experience: Metadata Tool Requirements

Metadata tools, like data catalogs and metadata repositories, benefit organizations in several ways. Benefits include improved abilities to discover and locate data, improved understanding of the data, improved governance and stewardship of data definition, production, and usage, and improved collaboration to improve the quality and value of the data.

When selecting a tool, it is important to identify technical and business requirements that will be used to match vendors and tools with the organization's needs. The business metadata requirements, or how business areas will use the metadata, are extremely valuable to the selection process. To learn more about your business requirements, consider using the previous essay to focus on defining the business questions that the metadata in your tool will need to answer.

We must also consider technical requirements when evaluating a tool's ability to demonstrate value. Ten categories of technical metadata tool requirements must be considered as part of the selection process, regardless of business requirements.

The categories are:

- Metamodels and Software Releases
- Extensibility
- Self-Defined Loads
- Role Representation
- Process Integration
- Change Control and Versioning
- Communications
- End User Navigation
- Training and Education
- Resource Requirements

This essay briefly describes ten technical metadata requirements to consider when selecting the appropriate metadata tool for your organization.

Metamodels and Software Releases

Metamodels are the logical and physical models that represent how the metadata is stored in the tool. Metamodels are often vendor- and product-specific, depending on how the metadata is represented in each tool. For example, a metamodel may vary from Database Management System (DBMS) to DBMS. The metadata for an Oracle database may differ from the metadata for an IBM database.

Vendors often reuse metadata and portions of metamodels maintained by their tools. For example, the physical database metamodel will reuse components of a physical database (i.e., database name, table name, column name, key) and the logical metamodel of a logical database design (entities, attributes, domains) for the different platforms they support.

The information in the metamodels will become important:

- if you will consider accessing the metadata with means other than through the tool itself
- if you will be developing your own metadata load capabilities
- if you will be developing your own reports against the metadata in the tools
- if you will be integrating metadata between tools and platform
- if you want to assess the quality of the metadata in the tool

Metamodels are often associated with releases or versions of the metadata tool. For example, when a product progresses from version to version, there are typically changes to the way the metadata is stored in the tool. The metamodels are updated to represent those changes.

Extensibility

Extensibility is the ability to add metadata categories and attributes to the out-of-box implementation of the metadata tool and incorporate them into existing metamodels and tool functionality. Extensibility becomes important when the tool does not precisely meet your needs or requirements. Extensions typically result in changes to the metamodels. Organizations typically maintain a development environment to create, test, and integrate the extended changes physically in the tool database. Metadata populating extensions to the tool typically require the direct ability to enter and maintain the metadata in the tool itself, or to create a customized (self-defined) load process (discussed next).

Self-Defined Loads

Self-defined loads is a term used to describe the ability to design and build customized processes to load metadata into the tool. Vendors typically provide the ability to load metadata from a finite number of tools in your environment through connectors that read from the metadata in these tools and insert the metadata properly in the data catalog or repository tool. These connectors may be included with the metadata tool or need to be purchased from a tool integrator. This is likely where most of your metadata will come from (other tools).

The ability to define and deploy a customized loading process is critical to controlling your ability to load metadata from places not supported by the metadata tool vendor quickly and easily.

Another reason these loads are important is that, even though you can purchase the "engine" to move metadata from a tool to the metadata tool, vendors often release new versions and releases of their software independently. The engine may cease functioning properly when the vendor changes how the metadata is stored in their tool. It often becomes a software "wait and see" approach to synchronizing the tool's ability to pass metadata between them. Therefore, defining and deploying self-defined loads becomes critical to keeping the metadata in the metadata tool current.

This feature or functionality relates closely to the extensibility function defined earlier in this essay. When the metadata tool is extended to include new information, the engines that function between tools do not populate the extensions. Or the extensions result in a category or subject area of metadata that cannot be loaded through traditional means. Therefore, the ability to write and maintain customized load functions becomes critical to loading metadata into the tool.

Role Representation

Role representation is the tool's ability to record people in roles defined as part of your data governance operating model of roles and responsibilities. Clearly defined accountability for data lies at the heart of your data governance program. This accountability must be for the data being governed as well as the metadata associated with that data. Metadata tools must be able to associate 1) a person to a role and 2) a role to a function of the tool.

Often, multiple people will play the same or similar roles in a data governance program. For example, all people using a specific type of data must abide by the same data protection, risk management, and quality rules. And a single person may participate in several roles. Therefore, it is important that 1) people can be associated with multiple roles and 2) that multiple roles can be associated with data, metadata, and processes simultaneously. It is important that the metadata tool can represent these relationships effectively.

Process Integration

Process integration is a term used to describe how the metadata tool can become part of daily activities associated with data and the governing of that data. The metadata in the tool will only become valuable if it is stored and used to make it easy for people to utilize that metadata to improve their efficiency and effectiveness of business operations. Therefore, it is important that the tools be integrated into business processes easily and effectively.

Process integration may include simple metadata processes such as adding new metadata, updating that metadata, and deleting metadata. Or the processes may be more complex, like providing data meaning and lineage along with data on a report, on a dashboard, on a screen, or providing the capability to coordinate the feedback process on new or refined data definitions. The ability to put the metadata in the hands of people is critical to metadata tool success.

Change Control and Versioning

Change control is an important requirement of metadata tool implementation. Both the manual and automated change control of the metadata in the tool is critical to the ongoing successful implementation and use of the tool. Without successful change control, the metadata that is stored in the tool becomes an image of the metadata at a point in time. For example, loading the data warehouse's database structure into the metadata tool is extremely important. However, keeping that information up to date when the data warehouse design evolves is critical to maintaining the current and high-quality metadata in the catalog or repository.

Versioning is also an important requirement of tool implementation. Recording and keeping records of changes to metadata become a valuable asset to the organization. Metadata tools must have effective capabilities to track the history of metadata changes.

Communications

The metadata tool's ability to improve communications associated with critical data becomes vital to getting the most out of the metadata tool. The metadata tool must provide the most basic of communications functions. These functions can be as simple as providing the information of the person to contact regarding a question about the data, or as complex as notifying all appropriate stakeholders that a rule associated with the data has changed.

End User Navigation

End-user requirements focus on the consumers' ability to traverse through the tool's metadata to find the information required to complete their job function. These requirements cover functions and operations that end-users recognize as essential to get the most out of the metadata tool.

Training and Education

Training and education must be provided to familiarize people with the metadata tool, its functionality, and how it can be used. Most vendors provide significant training to their customer base via different channels (for example, off-site, on-site, on-line/remote, and on-demand). Your organization must consider training and education in the metadata tool evaluation process.

Training and education are typically part of the purchase and maintenance price of the tool and must be considered as part of the total cost of ownership. Training and education must be considered for managing the product – including the installation, testing, development of test and production environments, maintenance and new releases of the tool, development, and synchronization of metadata connectors for moving metadata to and from the tool.

End-user training and education also become very important in implementing the tool. Providing the end user base with a solid foundation on data governance and metadata definition, production, and usage is important, as well as teaching them and refreshing them on tool access and functionality. On-going end-user support is also extremely important, not only when deploying the tool to technical and business users, but on a regular and as-needed basis.

Resource Requirements

Resource requirements are a technical critical success factor when investing in and implementing a metadata tool. Metadata tools require resources to achieve a successful and sustainable implementation. The number of required resources varies depending on the size of the organization and the size, breadth, goals, and expectations of the metadata implementation.

More often than not, having the resources required to implement and sustain a metadata tool becomes a key determining success factor. I often observe that companies operate with a very lean staff with people participating in many different roles. Therefore, it is critical that your organization thoroughly understand the resources required to get the most value and use out of their metadata tool.

The metadata tool vendor should be able to provide estimates of the required resources to deploy their tool and support the organization's technical and business communities. The vendor should be able to provide information based on similar implementations with expectations similar to those of your organization.

Key Messages

Most organizations recognize that business requirements play an important role in evaluating all software tools, specifically metadata tools. However, they may not recognize that these are not the only requirements to consider while evaluating tools and vendors.

This essay addressed a series of technical requirements that must also be considered when evaluating a tool's ability to demonstrate value. This essay briefly addressed ten categories of technical metadata tool requirements that must be considered as part of the tool selection process.

Perspective: Metadata Will Not Govern Itself Either

To close out this book, I am going to address a favorite topic of mine – Metadata Governance. Metadata governance is easiest to explain when you separate the term into two parts: metadata and data governance. Ask any organization that excels in metadata management whether or not they govern their metadata, and they will most certainly respond affirmatively. These organizations make certain that people are formally accountable for the metadata—because it is known that the metadata will not govern itself.

Formal accountability means that there are consequences for not taking the required actions. Formal accountability requires that the actions are documented and formalized by being included in a person's job description and the basis for performance evaluation. Some organizations shy away from the concept of formal accountability because it sounds invasive or over and above someone's existing level of accountability.

Accountability is often assumed but not formally enforced. It is the formal enforcement of guidelines and rules that feels threatening to individuals and to the organization. My experience with the non-invasive approach to data governance has demonstrated that organizations should consider only formalizing accountability for actions that the organization must ensure are taking place. Formal accountability for additional actions will begin to feel invasive.

Most of the accountabilities required for data must also be applied to metadata. To ensure high-quality and timely metadata, people must be formally accountable for defining the metadata that is important to the organization, for producing the metadata, and for using the metadata. Data governance programs must focus on directing these people's actions to ensure that metadata is being defined, produced, and used consistently.

A metadata steward, like a typical data steward, is someone that defines, produces, and/or uses metadata as part of their job and is being held formally accountable for the actions they take with metadata. These people are critical to your metadata management and metadata governance efforts.

The concept of governing metadata, or formally managing data documentation, may be new to your organization. Therefore, the governance of metadata may be viewed as being over and above or invasive in terms of governance. To address this perception, building the activities of defining, producing, and using metadata in people's present job functions and procedures becomes necessary.

Governing the definition of metadata means that there is formal accountability for selecting the appropriate metadata that needs to be governed. This action includes providing usable descriptions of the metadata, why it is important, and how it can and should be used. Governing metadata definition includes providing guidelines and standards for the metadata that will be produced and used and monitoring requirements for additional metadata that will be governed.

Governing the production of metadata means that there is enforced accountability for creating and maintaining metadata. This includes an assurance that metadata will be produced at the appropriate time and in the appropriate location following the specific guidelines and standards associated with that category of metadata. Guidelines and standards associated with metadata production focus on the accuracy, completeness, consistency, and timeliness of the metadata.

Governing the use of metadata means that there is formalized and enforced accountability for using the metadata to ensure that the actions people take with data are appropriate, compliant, responsible, and ethical. Governing the use of metadata ensures that the rules associated with using the data and metadata are shared along with the data.

Consider gamifying your metadata governance initiatives to make the actions of governing metadata feel less threatening or invasive. I spelled out four approaches to gamifying data governance in an earlier essay. For example, measuring the engagement of data stewards and metadata stewards as they participate in governing data and metadata.

Also, consider automating the definition, production, and usage of metadata as much as possible to decrease your levels of reliance on the metadata stewards. Metadata automation requires that you know where and when the metadata is being produced, when changes are occurring, how the metadata changes will be reflected in your metadata tools, who will be notified of the changes to the metadata, and that you automate metadata processes when changes to metadata occur.

Organizations recognize that data documentation and metadata play an important role in the governance and management of data. Automating metadata definition, production, and usage processes will become increasingly important as organizations leverage the information and metadata they have about their data.

Key Messages

Without automation, you will depend on your metadata stewards to define, produce, and use your metadata. The quality of the definition, production, and usage of your metadata will be an important factor in your data management and data governance effort's success.

Activate your metadata stewards to improve the likelihood that your metadata management effort will be successful. There is no magical solution to the governance of metadata and the delivery of high-value metadata. Lack of formal metadata actions will lead to low levels of confidence and trust in your organization's data. The metadata will not govern itself.

Index

Agile, 70, 73, 231

Algmin, Anthony, 241

atomic, 46, 47

auditor, 39

authority, 10, 11, 13, 18, 19, 21, 22, 26, 29, 32, 34, 68, 71, 73, 74, 75, 78, 85, 111, 134, 136, 160, 163, 165, 171, 172, 173, 174, 181, 182, 193, 196, 197, 205, 206, 215, 217, 219, 227, 235, 236, 238, 239, 249, 262, 263, 268

BERT, 252

big data, 22, 32, 34, 66, 124, 145, 171, 172, 204, 226, 231, 264

business glossaries, 33, 129, 136, 163, 166, 227, 231, 233, 266, 270

business intelligence, 11, 24, 36, 66, 175, 233, 242

Capability Maturity Model, 49

Carnegie Mellon University, 49

cause and effect, 141, 142, 143

CDAO. See Chief Data and Analytics Officer

CDE. See Critical Data Elements

CDO. See Chief Data Officer

CFO. See Chief Financial Officer

ChatGPT, 252

Chief Data and Analytics Officer, 77, 167, 168, 242

Chief Data Officer, 77, 100, 150, 167, 168

Chief Financial Officer, 167, 219

Chief Information Officer, 78

Chief Information Security Officer, 150, 168

Chief Operational Officer, 167

Chief Privacy Officer, 167

Chief Risk Officer, 167

CIO. See Chief Information Officer

CISO. See Chief Information Security Officer

CMM. See Capability Maturity Model

collaborative, 10, 118

command-and-control, 1, 38, 39, 41, 42, 43, 44, 101, 102

Common Data Matrix, 205

communications, 19, 20, 21, 26, 29, 30, 60, 65, 75, 123, 146, 150, 161, 163, 166, 173, 182, 183, 204, 215, 220, 221, 249, 276

communications plan, 21, 29, 163, 166, 220

controller, 206, 207

COO. See Chief Operational Officer

CPO. See Chief Privacy Officer

Critical Data Element, 114

CRM. See Customer Relationship Management

CRO. See Chief Risk Officer

Customer Relationship Management, 204

data analytics, 58, 84

data anarchy, 68, 69, 71

data apocalypse, 79, 82

data architecture, 175, 211, 212, 216

data babysitter, 91

data catalogs, 33, 129, 136, 166, 227, 231, 272

data classification, 26, 198, 206

Data Czar, 100

data definer, 35, 196, 198

data definitions, 21, 31, 89, 113, 189, 276

data demon, 72, 73, 75

data dictionaries, 33, 129, 136, 163, 166, 227, 231, 233, 266, 270

data documentation, 174, 227, 245

Data Domain Steward, 18, 185

data fabric, 46, 261, 262, 263

data flu, 77, 78

data governance, 243
  explanation of, 10–12
  maturity levels for, 50–54
  puzzle for, 59–65
  six mistakes of, 144–47
  value of, 128–32

Data Governance Administrator, 169

Data Governance Council, 17, 26, 183, 184, 187, 188

Data Governance Framework, 13, 14, 15, 16, 17, 19, 23, 38, 173

Data Governance Manager, 30, 182, 184, 185, 186, 187, 189, 210

data governance maturity levels, 50–54

Data Governance Office, 160

Data Governance Partner, 182

data governance process, 20, 27, 28, 36, 43, 118

data governance purpose, 243

data governance puzzle, 59–65

data governance six mistakes, 144–47

data governance team, 28, 30, 52, 53, 144, 169

data governance value, 128–32

Data Governance Working Team, 182, 184, 185, 186, 187, 189

data integration, 11, 36, 70

data intervention, 83, 84, 85, 86, 87

Data Intervention Team Leader, 84

data leadership, 241

data management, 2, 46, 48, 50, 54, 58, 83, 85, 100, 143, 144, 149, 150, 171, 173, 174, 175, 176, 177, 216, 226, 230, 231, 263

data mesh, 46, 261, 262, 263, 264

Data Owner, 18

data production steward, 74, 195, 204

data sanitizer, 76

data situation, 56, 57, 58, 79, 80, 82, 84, 85, 148, 149, 150

data steward, 1, 18, 27, 35, 36, 60, 88, 89, 90, 172, 174, 191, 195, 196, 198, 200, 201, 202, 203, 204, 206, 207, 208, 209, 244, 279

data stewardship, 25, 90, 174, 191, 219, 235, 261, 268

data strategy, 56, 57, 58, 84, 148

Data Subject Matter Steward, 185, 187, 188

data warehousing, 66, 233

Database Management System, 273

data-centric, 75, 84, 130, 132, 134, 149

data-enabled, 130
data-savvy, 130
DBMS. See Database Management System
deputy, 114
DGA. See Data Governance Administrator
DGO. See Data Governance Office
Doctor of Data, 77
domain-focused quality, 31
Enterprise Data Steward, 18
Enterprise Resource Planning, 204
ERP. See Enterprise Resource Planning
examiner, 39
Excel, 162, 164
executive, 13, 17, 24, 25, 26, 28, 29, 31, 32, 65, 75, 120, 136, 149, 168, 181, 182, 206, 219, 220, 236
executive level, 17, 24, 25, 28, 29, 31, 32, 181, 182, 206, 236
Fast Company, 92
federated, 149, 160, 161, 162, 164, 166
framework, 13, 14, 15, 16, 18, 19, 21, 24, 29, 33, 38, 41, 65, 121, 122, 169, 175, 176, 188, 210, 211
FTE. See Full-Time-Equivalent
Full-Time-Equivalent, 205
Gaddis, William, 81
Gartner, 78
go-to person, 18
GPT-3, 252
high-quality data, 21, 31, 57, 85, 191, 245
HR. See Human Resources
Human Resources, 19, 182, 189, 206, 215, 218
Information Governance, 24, 40, 42

information security, 19, 27, 28, 150, 176, 217, 236, 249
Information Technology, 19, 33, 36, 167, 215, 216, 244
Intellectual Property, 150
IP. See Intellectual Property
issue resolution, 20, 21, 27, 29, 30, 43, 163, 165, 197
IT. See Information Technology
key performance indicator, 48
KPI. See key performance indicator
Large Language Model, 252
legal and audit, 19
LLM. See Large Language Model
low-hanging fruit, 63
Magic Kingdom, 57
Master Data Management, 36, 204, 226
MDM. See Master Data Management
Messages for Management, 2
metadata categories, 265–70
metadata governance, 24, 171, 172, 280
metadata management, 165, 175, 231
metadata plan, 264
methodologies, 11, 36
NIDG. See Non-Invasive Data Governance
Non-Invasive Data Governance, 1, 2, 10, 11, 12, 13, 15, 16, 17, 19, 23, 24, 34, 35, 36, 37, 38, 40, 41, 67, 88, 117, 118, 122, 145, 173, 203, 204, 205, 208
operational level, 18, 28, 30, 31, 33, 75, 181, 183, 228
Oracle, 273
Pandora's Box, 57

partner, 25, 182, 215, 216, 217, 218, 220

People, Process, and Technology, 133, 134

Personal Health Information, 150

Personally Identifiable Information, 150

PHI. See Personal Health Information

PII. See Personally Identifiable Information

PMO. See Project Management Office

privacy, 11, 36, 248, 249

producer, 35, 89, 149, 161, 162, 164, 196, 199

Project Management Office, 19, 215, 221

project methodology, 43, 189, 231

public policy, 235, 236

quantifiable, 21, 30, 114

Ready, Aim, Fire, 229

ready, fire, aim, 61

records, 19, 23, 24, 25, 42, 101, 176, 217, 276

records management, 24

re-playable, 59

request for access, 43, 163, 165

Return on Investment, 39, 44, 145

right-sizing, 17

risk management, 11, 27, 34, 36, 134, 167, 182, 217, 249, 275

Robinson, Eleanor, 59

ROI. See Return on Investment

Roles and Responsibilities, 13, 20, 25, 180, 190, 205

Rooney, Andy, 81

same difference, 173

second-in-command, 17

Shakespeare, William, 195

SharePoint, 162, 164

shelf-ware, 51

smart data, 22, 32, 66, 145

SME. See Subject Matter Expert

Software Engineering Institute, 49

standard operating procedures, 11, 36

steering committee, 17, 26

strategic level, 17, 18, 26, 28, 29, 31, 32, 33, 69, 123, 169, 181, 182, 183, 196, 206, 218

strategic planning, 60, 61

structured data, 23, 42, 232

Subject Matter Expert, 28, 212

supportive, 10, 118

tactical level, 18, 25, 28, 30, 31, 33, 181, 183, 185, 205, 246

taxonomy, 174

The National Review Magazine, 93

top-down, 39, 43, 101

traditional, 38, 39, 40, 42, 43, 44, 45, 101, 102

transformation, 52, 133, 135, 175, 212, 213, 232, 261, 263

transparent, 10, 118

unstructured data, 23, 24, 25, 40, 42, 172

Visio, 162, 164

Washington Post, 93

wikiHow, 86

workflow, 33, 36

www.ingramcontent.com/pod-product-compliance
Lightning Source LLC
Chambersburg PA
CBHW081805200326

41597CB00023B/4155